The Selected Works of J.R. Campbell
First Prism Key Press Edition 2011

Prism Key Press
New York, NY 10001
PrismKeyPress.com

ISBN-13: 978-1468051766

The Selected Works of J.R. Campbell

CONTENTS

Leninism and the Party

One of the most important features of Lenin's teaching is that concerning the role of a revolutionary party in the struggles of the workers. Lenin's theory, based upon a long experience of the Labour Movement, comes up against not only the principles advocated by the Social-Democracy, but also those advocated by certain Marxian (?) schools in Great Britain.

The existing moderate Socialist parties attained their greatest development in the years before the war, when capitalism was expanding and the profits of colonial robbery were flowing in a steady stream into the hands of the big capitalists in the leading capitalist countries. Those capitalists were able to grant a number of social reforms to the workers and to spread amongst them the illusion of a steady progress, under capitalism, to a greater state of well-being.

As a consequence of this development there arose in the Socialist Movement the "Revisionist" school who contended that the Marxian analysis was wrong, that capitalism was not moving to a crisis, and that the class struggle so far from intensifying was softening down.

Phrasemongers

This Revisionist doctrine was never fully accepted by the Continental Socialist parties in theory. In their programmes Marxist doctrine continued to have a place of honour allotted to them. Marxist phrases were widely used in speeches and in the press. The practice of these parties, however, were completely revisionist. *Thus there was in the Social-Democratic Parties a complete disharmony between theory and practice.*

As the parties were mainly concerned with getting electoral majorities, the question of discipline was naturally a secondary one. Groups with the most diverse views of Socialist theory and policy sheltered under the same expansive Social-Democratic umbrella. *The result was that the Social-Democratic parties contained groups and schools waging continuous war against each other. There was no ideological unity.*

Against this method of party organisation Lenin waged unrelenting war. The conditions in Russia were such that only a disciplined party, ideologically united under strong central direction, harmonising theory with practice, could lead the workers in the struggle.

This idea of the role of a party was naturally more acceptable in Russia, where the workers were organising and struggling illegally, than in the countries of Western Europe, in which Liberal ideas had infected the Labour Movement.

Since the war, however, the expansion of Western European capitalism has stopped. It is no longer able to throw sops at the workers, but it can only live by intensifying their exploitation and their misery.

We are therefore in Western Europe also entering upon a period of mass struggle leading up to the conquest of power.

One only requires to envisage the problem of bringing large masses into the struggle effectively to realise that unless those masses are under the influence of a trained and disciplined leadership their efforts will be sporadic, chaotic, and aimless.

A Communist Party is a party, embracing or aspiring to embrace all the advanced members of the working class. It incarnates the collective experience of the working class gained in the struggle against capitalism. Such a party must be closely linked up with the workers, understanding their problems, sensing their moods, and assisting, them in the every-day struggle. It is fatal for a workers' party to pursue a policy which does not take into consideration the state of mind of the masses.

It must be in contact not with the more active workers in

the trade union branches and the Local Labour Parties, but must also be in contact with the masses of workers in the workshop. (Hence factory groups.)

A revolutionary party must, however, lead the workers. It must not allow itself to be dragged along by the masses, but must understand the development of events, give its lead to the workers in order that their struggle can be waged in the most effective and revolutionary fashion. *It must become the political leader of the working class.*

It is worth mentioning that Lenin had, in building the Bolshevik party, to combat a theory similar to one which has been widely spread in Marxist circles in Britain, though it has never been given a name. It was called by Lenin the theory of "spontaneity" *and its essence is that it neglects or despises the role that a revolutionary party plays in the struggles of the workers.* We have all met its British protagonists.

Automatic Revolution

"Conditions," they tell us "are becoming more acute; they will force the workers to act as a class; the workers will spontaneously throw up the necessary organisation and leadership to enable them to conduct the struggles." Often the protagonists of this theory (who include, all sorts of people from anti-parliamentarians to left wing members of the Labour Party) assert that the theoretical divergences in the movement do not matter much, because they will be sorted out and tested "when the crisis comes."

This theory is widely held by people who look at the Labour Movement from outside. Movements that appear to them to be spontaneous are often actually movements which have been carefully prepared and organised by active groups.

It should be plain to any worker that mass movements have to be capably prepared and carefully handled. This can only be done by a party which combines a correct theory of

9

society with the utmost ability and experience in applying its theory to the everyday struggle of the masses, and the utmost willingness to recast its tactics in the light of experience.

Leninism is the application of Marxism to the problems confronting the workers in the period of Imperialist capitalism, and to the problems of socialist reconstruction where the capitalists have been overthrown. It is not a final theory, but a theory capable of amplification in the light of knowledge gained in the struggle of the workers.

The Communist parties move in the light of Leninism. Unlike the parties of the Second International they are ideologically united.

A revolutionary party must also be organised itself. It must learn to move sharply in response to a Communist lead, and to move as a united body.

This necessitates an iron discipline and a capable centralized leadership

It is this feature of organisation of Communist Parties which provokes unrestrained Menshevik merriment. The Communist is represented as an individual with no mind of his own. The Presidium of the Comintern is supposed to give out the most detailed orders. These orders are accepted by E.C. of the Communist Parties in the various countries who do not criticise but pass them humbly to the membership, and the membership being "slaves of Moscow" duly carry them out.

Now as a matter of plain fact there is more political discussion in a Communist Party in a week than there, is in a Menshevik organisation in a year. The membership are entitled to express their opinion and do express it upon the policy of the International. Have not the same Mensheviks constantly sneered at the Communists for continually discussing theses? And are not our theses simply documents laying down views of the political line of the party and the International?

Discussion and Discipline

There is the fullest discussion on the main lines of policy in a Communist Party, but when these lines have been determined, there is no need to discuss every detail of tactical application while one is engaged in the heat of the struggle. Tactics have to be applied quickly, but after a certain line of tactics has been applied the question of whether it was correct or not can be opened.

That then is the Communist theory of the role of the party in the struggles of the workers, and it follows from it as clearly as night follows day that there are no Communists outside the Communist Party, because adherence to Communism means not only acceptance of a theory which gives the party a role of tremendous importance in the workers' struggle, but it also means the application of that theory in daily life.

Such a being as an "unorganised revolutionary" is a political monstrosity.

Without the training of work within the ranks of a Communist Party, one may be a sympathiser (and then there is hope) or a political dilettante (and in this there is damnation), but one is not a revolutionist.

That is the teaching of Leninism. Can any left winger or non-party Marxist dispute it?

Were the Miners Let Down?

THE publication, by Mr. John Bromley, in the *Locomotive Journal* of extracts from the report which was to have been presented by the General Council to the meeting of Trade Union Executives called for June 25, has at last given the working class an opportunity of examining the reasons for the conduct of the General Council during the recent General Strike.

The extracts from the report of the General Council, in the article in question, are mixed up with rhetorical and, in some cases, hysterical interpolations emanating from Mr. Bromley himself. Some of these interpolations have been seized upon by the Capitalist Press as representing the considered opinion of the General Council, an action against which the General Council may have protested by the time this article appears in print.

In examining the General Council's case we have gone over the article exceedingly carefully, have excluded anything which might be regarded as an interpolation by Mr. Bromley, have endeavoured to give the General Council the benefit of the doubt in every doubtful instance, and yet the only result is that in considering the bare quotations from the Report itself we are led to the conclusion that the General Council's apology constitutes the most damning indictment of a leadership in the history of the Trade Union Movement of this country.

In order to approach the discussion in a realistic way, it is necessary to ask ourselves what is behind the attack on miners' wages and hours. Is this attack due to the fact that the mining industry, owing to bad management and to circumstances over which it had no control, got into a difficult position, while the rest of British Industry is moving along in a perfectly satisfactory fashion?

In other words, is the crisis which provoked the attack

on miners' wages a mining industry crisis, or a crisis in British Capitalism?

Any intelligent worker will agree that what we are faced wife at the present moment is a crisis in British Capitalism; that not only in the mining industry, but in the basic industries of the country also, there is a condition of absolute stagnation.

Out of this stagnation the employers only see one way, "The wages of all workers must come down." We need not remind the readers of the LABOUR MONTHLY that the mining employers attacked the miners' wages in the summer of 1925 at a time when the wages of the workers in the metal and cotton industries and on the railways were also being challenged. The victory of "Red Friday" stopped the capitalist offensive elsewhere except for the slight worsening of conditions forced upon the railwaymen, but no one with any intelligence could possibly doubt that if the miners go down in the present struggle the wages of all other workers will be attacked also.

It is shameful to be forced to occupy the space of the LABOUR MONTHLY in stressing this elementary fact. We do it not for the benefit of the rank and file who have grasped it long ago, but for the benefit of the General Council who had not apparently grasped it during the period of the General Strike. The whole case of the General Council in its Report to the Conference of Executives is based on the assumption that the workers in other unions who supported the miners were merely nobly and self-sacrificingly engaging in sympathetic action on behalf of the miners, whereas the truth of the matter is that they were engaged in resisting a mass attack of the capitalists directed not merely against the miners but against themselves.

This offensive of the capitalists was prepared openly under the noses of the Trade Union leadership. The recruitment of the O.M.S. and of special constabulary, the establishment of emergency strike-breaking machinery, were all undertaken in the open, and ought to have convinced the dullest individual that the Government was preparing to back the employers in a mass attack upon the working class. No one will dispute that the O.M.S. and the emergency preparations generally were weapons of the capitalists against the workers. What the General Council has not yet grasped is that the Coal Commission were equally a weapon of the offensive against the working class. Unless we believe that the present Government is composed of madmen, it is impossible to conceive of them at one and the same time setting up emergency machinery to be used against the workers and setting up a Coal Commission to be used against the employers. Obviously, the Coal Commission, as its wholly capitalist composition showed, was a weapon of the capitalist offensive.

The case against the General Council is that it refused to prepare against the O.M.S. strike-breaking weapon of the Government, and that it absolutely succumbed to the Coal Commission strike-breaking weapon of the Government. In all the months between the granting of the subsidy and the issue of the Coal Commission Report, the General Council refused to elaborate any consistent wage policy to be pursued in relation to the mining dispute. The reason for this was obvious. Nothing that the Coal Commission could do could alter the basic facts of the mining industry, namely that present wages could not be paid without either the adoption of a drastic system of nationalisation and unification without compensation, or by a continuation of the subsidy. Both of these methods of retaining mining wages were ignored because both of them involved a challenge to the normal principles on which capitalist industry is carried on, and involved preparation to bring pressure to bear on the Government.

The result of their refusal to adopt a consistent wage policy was that the General Council simply drifted along, hoping that the Report of the Coal Commission which the Government intended to use as a weapon against the miners would in some miraculous way turn out to be a weapon directed against the mineowners and the capitalist offensive.

The development of this policy is clearly outlined in the General Council's document. On February 26, the Industrial Committee of the T.U.C. made a declaration in favour of no reductions in wages, no increase in hours and no interference with the principle of national agreements in the mining industry. On March 10, the Coal Commission issued its report which proved to be, as all intelligent rank and file workers expected it to be, a weapon directed- against the miners and the working class. The General Council, afraid to enter into a struggle, persuaded themselves that this report was of value to the miners and their whole as policy from the issue of the Report was one of forcing its acceptance upon the miners' leaders.

On April 8, the miners asked the Industrial Committee of he General Council to give again a declaration in favour of no reductions in wages, no increase in hours, and national agreements, The Industrial Committee refused to do so. In conveying its decision to A. J. Cook in a letter of April 8, Mr. Citrine said that the Industrial Committee was "of the opinion that matters have not yet reached a stage when any final declaration of the Genera! Council's policy can be made."

Here we have a piquant situation. The Government grants a subsidy to enable preparations to be made to defeat the miners as a preliminary to defeating the working class. It appoints a Col Commission which presents a Report that will facilitate the defeat of the workers. The General Council accepts this defeatist Report and lines up with the Government of the capitalist class in endeavouring to force its acceptance on the miners! Only one thing prevented the success of this project, and that was that the mineowners' demands went far beyond the demands for reductions in wages in the Commission's Report, and forced the General Council for the time being to make a gesture on behalf of the miners. In making the gesture of solidarity by calling the General Strike on May 1, the General Council was endeavouring to bluff the Government. Bluff may sometimes justify itself in industrial warfare, but only upon the condition that those who are bluffing do not give the game away beforehand. The General Council had shown during the interval between May 1 and May 3 that it was prepared to force reductions in wages on the miners.

It made this attitude quite clear to the Government in accepting from Mr. Baldwin on May 2, the formula which it considered to be worthy of acceptance by the miners. The formula read as follows:—

The Prime Minister has satisfied himself that as a result of conversations he had with representatives of the T.U.C., if negotiations are continued, it being understood that the notices cease to be operative, the representatives of the T.U.C. are confident that a settlement could be reached along the lines of the Report within a fortnight.

Obviously, the most cowardly Capitalist Government that ever existed would be strengthened in its determination to fight the workers by the spectacle of the leaders on the workers' side absolutely running away. Thus the General Council encouraged the Government to take up a strong attitude by its open display of weakness.

The Government felt that with such leaders the whole struggle would be over in a few days, the mining dispute included, and that as a result it was worth while calling the bluff.

When the General Strike took place, it took place with this leadership having no hope of victory. Dealing with the perspectives of the strike the General Council says:—

From the position, therefore, taken up by the Government through their ultimatum, there appeared to be only two alternatives; the capitulation of the

Government; the disintegration of the strike by a process of attrition. It was clear that the Government would use their majority in the House and the utmost resources available to them to maintain the position they had taken up.

In other words, the General Council went through the strike with only one idea, *i.e.*, that the Government was impregnable, that nothing that the working class could do would shake its determination and therefore the strike ought to be called off at the first opportunity.

It has been freely said by its apologists since that no strike can possibly succeed which is directed against the Government. This is an idea which is hopelessly defeatist. All great struggles in our basic industries must under present conditions bring in the Government. The only way to avoid bringing the Government into an industrial dispute is either to assent to the reductions in wages imposed by the capitalists, or to conduct a fight in a sectional fashion and so produce defeat. If the workers are seriously concerned for the future, however, they will not waste their time in sectional struggles, but will bring all their forces to bear at the one moment. When this happens the Government is immediately bound to interfere and strike back. A strike is a political weapon. This only means, however, that in modern industry, any effective struggle of the working class to preserve their standards must come up against the Capitalist State, which is not the representative of the community, but is simply the principal employing-class weapon in the struggle against the workers' standards. A courageous leadership recognising this would have gone all out to win. The case against the General Council is that it did not develop or attempt to develop the struggle so as to bring the full forces of the workers to bear.

It is worthy of note in this connection that most of the right wing leaders on the Continent could only explain the calling off of the strike by the General Council on the basis of mass strike breaking and a mass return to work. Even the Continental Amsterdam leaders failed to discover any reason why the strike should have been called off when the workers were still solid.

With regard to the Samuel Memorandum, which the General Council accepted as a basis of settlement, the Report does not claim for the memorandum any official Government connection but merely states that it is a good basis for settlement and that if the miners had accepted it as basis for negotiations, public opinion would haw forced the Government to accept it also. We do not wish to quarrel with this statement, because we believe that the Samuel Memorandum, while a bad basis of settlement for the miners and the working class, is a good basis of settlement for the capitalist class. It asks the miners to place their destiny with regard to wages anti conditions in the hands of an independent chairman of a National Wages Board. In other words, it sees as the solution of the wages problem in the coal industry the appointment of a capitalist arbitrator. What would have happened to the miners' wages if they had been fools enough to accept can readily be imagined.

Were the miners correct in refusing to accept reductions in wages? Both from their own point of view as miners, and from the point of view of the wider interests of the working class, they were undoubtedly correct. Nothing would be more likely to encourage the capitalists of other industries to attack the workers than an easy acceptance of wage cuts in an industry which has always been regarded as a stronghold of Trade Unionism.

The insistance of the miners has already ensured that any victory gained by the capitalist class is going to be ten times more costly than the granting of a subsidy would have been. Even when wage cuts are inevitable it is always good Trade Union policy to "die hard," thereby preventing the development of the offensive on a wider scale. As a matter of fact, however, wage cuts in the mining industry are not inevitable and given proper support to the miners even at the present moment by means of the imposition of an embargo on coal, nationally and internationally, wage cuts could be avoided and a subsidy extracted from the capitalists for a further period.

Mr. John Bromley in presenting the Report deals with a further aspect of the matter which is well worth considering from the working-class standpoint. He says —

> To have adopted the slogan of the miners' leaders would, on their own admission, if accepted, have meant the immediate throwing out of work of some 300,000 mine workers by the closing of uneconomic mines, which appears too awful for any Trade Union leaders to contemplate. For to many thinking people it is bound to appear more sane for some highly paid men in a disorganised industry to suffer some temporary reduction than to throw 300,000 workers and their families into destitution so that a number of men earning on the admission of Mr. Cook, the Miners' Secretary, from £5 to £13 per week may retain every penny of their present wages.

It ought to be clear to every trade unionist that Mr. Bromley and such members of the General Council as agree with him in advocating this policy are challenging the everyday principles upon which the Trade Union Movement has hitherto conducted its wage struggles. It has always been the policy of the Trade Union Movement, even in its most reformist phases, to base its demands for wages upon what the most efficient business operating in any particular industry can pay. If the less efficient businesses are not able to pay the wages, then they have either got to make themselves more efficient or go out of the job. We are reaching a sorry pass in the British Labour Movement when it is being forced to adapt its minimum wage demands to the conditions of the uneconomic firms in a given industry. What this policy means any worker can grasp. It means starvation wages for the workers, and the preservation of parasitic, inefficient firms earning what is regarded as reasonable profits, while the up-to-date firms earn profits beyond the dreams of avarice.

Surely the sane policy to be adopted, even from the ordinary Trade Union standpoint, is the miners' policy of basing the minimum wage on what the most efficient firms and coalfields can pay, while a subsidy is being paid to enable wages to be maintained pending the reorganisation of the more inefficient firms.

That, we suggest, is the way to make minimum demands, as any trade unionist will agree who regards Trade Unionism as an instrument for maintaining the workers' standards, and not an instrument to co-operate with the employers to secure the progressive reduction of the standards of the workers.

Since issuing its apology the General Council has sent a circular calling for assistance for the miners and pointing out that we are now in the presence of a capitalist attack on the whole working class. We hope that the General Council realises that the admission of this fact reduces the apology for its conduct in the dispute to absolute nonsense.

The one lesson that we must draw from the whole situation is the inevitability of the continuation of the capitalist offensive, and of fresh struggles on the part of the workers if they are to maintain their standards. To conduct these struggles successfully a new leadership is required. The failure of the Trade Union "left" among the leaders was the failure of men who had not thought out their problems; who did not understand the nature of the situation they were facing, nor the methods which the working class would have to adopt to meet that situation. They were weak compared with the right wing, because the right wing in the person of Mr. Thomas has at least a policy—although it is one of treachery to the working class—and the ability to consistently pursue that policy through all its phases in a changing situation. Mr. Thomas knows his mind perfectly. The left-wing did not know their minds at all. The greatest lesson of the General Strike, therefore, is the need for a new leadership, who will study the complex problems arising out of the situation of British Capitalism, who will face temporary unpopularity and abuse in order to equip the British Labour Movement to face the changed situation and who in every struggle will go out to win, knowing no loyalty except loyalty to the working-class movement.

Communism and the Industrial Peace

The average worker who has never studied Communism must be confused as to the role which the Communist Party is playing in the British Labour movement at the present day.

Let us say he is a miner or an engineering worker. He may come in contact with a Communist in the same pit or engineering shop. He notices that this Communist is continually propagating his ideas, and is prepared to tale the lead in any struggle on behalf of the workers that may arise in the workshop or in the pit. Our miner or engineering worker may not understand all that the Communist stands for, but will probably arrive at the general conclusion that the Communist is a good fighter on the side of the working class. Later, he may read a report in the Press of a speech by Sir William Joynson-Hacks, denouncing the "Reds," and if he is a good labour man, will probably come to the conclusion that anything that Sir William Joynson-Hicks denounces is worthy of working-class support, and that therefore the Communists are a section of the working class who ought, to be encouraged.

He gets a shock, however, when, a few days later, he reads the account of a Labour Party Conference where the Communists are expelled because their policy is alleged to be inimical to the best interests of the working-class movement. If he reads the report of that conference he will find the Labour leaders denouncing the Communist Party in almost the same terms as Sir William Joynson-Hicks. The average worker will be naturally dumbfounded at this strange spectacle of Labour leaders and Tory Cabinet Ministers, who are alleged to be the sworn enemies of the Labour leaders, uniting to denounce the Communist Party. At the one moment the worker sees the Communist being victimised by the boss in the workshop, and at the next moment by the Right wing in the Local Labour Party, and is naturally led to wonder what strange kind of political party the Communist Party is when it draws the fire of the Labour leaders on the one hand and the leaders of the capitalist class on the other hand.

If our worker follows the Labour and capitalist Press, he finds Communism treated in different ways at different times. In the first place, he will find in both the capitalist Press and the Labour press, Communism treated as a joke. He will be told that the Communist movement has no influence in Great Britain whatsoever, and is worthy only of contempt. Yet the same papers — Labour and capitalist — which tell him that Communism is a joke and that it is unworthy of notice, are constantly giving it notice from week to week. At other times the Communist movement is treated as a menace, and the Press is full of scares about the machinations of the "Reds." The same Labour leaders who, a few months previously, have dismissed Communism as a joke, now begin to denounce loudly Communist intrigues in the Labour movement, and no less a person than the secretary of the Trade Union Congress, Mr. W. M. Citrine, commences a series of articles in a Labour paper in order to combat the growing menace of Communism in the Trade Union movement.

Our worker finds the Labour leaders deriding the Communists because they are alleged to believe in dictatorship and not in democracy. Yet he finds that some Labour leaders are combating Communist propaganda in their unions, not by democratic methods, but by depriving Communists of all rights within the Trade Union movement. He finds Communists attacked because they are bloodthirsty people working for a bloody upheaval. He may be impressed by this charge until he remembers that the people who most often level it against the Communists are people like Mr. Churchill or Labour leaders who served in the Coalition Government during the period of the war.

It would be quite impossible to answer all the lies which have been levelled against Communism in a pamphlet, or, for

24

that matter, in a whole library. Not by pamphlets alone, but also by daily experience in the class struggle, will the workers be won for Communism. Yet a pamphlet may be useful in removing prejudices, in inducing workers to study the question further, and particularly to realise that Communism is not merely the propagation of an ideal order of society, not merely the longing for a revolution which may come in the sweet bye and bye, but it is the political creed which affords to the worker the only practical guide to the successful waging of the day-to-day struggle against the capitalist class, and the development of that struggle towards the overthrow of capitalism.

The average worker is aware that all the political parties which claim his support have a programme which they put before him, explaining their point of view in relation to present-day questions. The Liberal has one programme, the Conservative another, and the Labour Party has another. Like all these political parties, the Communist Party has also a programme which it puts before the working class. Back of all these programmes, however, there exists in the mind of those who are propagating them a particular point of view as to the nature of present-day society and of the tendencies of present-day society. If the Conservative programme is different from the Communist programme it is because the Conservative programme represents the interests of a different class from that of the Communist Party. It represents the programme of the capitalist class which looks at present-day society from a different point of view from that of the working class, whose aspirations the Communist Party represent. In order to understand that attitude of the Communists towards present-day questions, it is therefore necessary to understand the Communist point of view in relation to present-day society.

If we look at the production of wealth in present-day society, we find that that production of wealth can only take place through the co-operation of many diverse trades and industries interlocked one with the other. Within a given workshop, the whole variety of workers, manual and mental,

25

co-operate together in order to produce a common product. Within society as a whole all industries co-operate together in order to produce wealth, the raw material of one industry being the finished product of the other. Without this co-operation of all the useful elements of society in production, there can be no society as we understand it to-day. Wealth to-day can only be produced and industry maintained through this co-operation.

The vast industries in which men co-operate to produce wealth to-day are not the creation of any particular class, but have only been created and can only be maintained by the co-operative labour of all useful elements in society. The technical knowledge, the science which is utilised by these industries is not the creation of any particular social class, but is the common product of men co-operating together in society.

This technical knowledge, this application of science to industry, is constantly increasing, and with it, the power to produce wealth quickly and efficiently. Within the lifetime of comparatively young men and women, we have seen tremendous progress in the application of science to industry. The use of electricity as a motive force in industry, the development of the motor-car from the wheezy machine which broke down every half mile, to the smooth running cars of to-day, the development of aviation, the application of oil fuel to industry, are all technical changes which have taken place within the lifetime of most of the readers of this pamphlet. The ability to produce wealth grows every year, and with it, in a rational system of society, the welfare of the mass of the people should grow also.

In capitalist society the opposite process is taking place. Alongside growing power to produce wealth there is growing poverty. According, to the Ministry of Health figures there were twice as many people on Poor Relief in 1924 as pre-war.

The wealth which is produced by the co-operative labour of all active workers in industry is divided in most hopelessly unequal fashion. The following table gives a good example of

26

how wealth is distributed in present-day society, giving one class enormous wealth and power and condemning the majority of the workers to poverty and subjection.

Distribution of National Income in 1923

Rent	£380,000,000
Interest	£840,000,000
Profits and Salaries	£820,000,000
Interest	£840,000,000
Total	£2,040,000,000
Income of Manual Workers	£1,360,000,000
Total	£3,400,000,000

In addition to this, the existing powers of wealth production are not being utilised to their fullest capacity. On the one hand, we have had for the past seven years, a huge unemployed army, never falling below the million mark. Alongside this army of unemployed workers there are idle factories and uncultivated land. Capitalist economists and Labour leaders talk as if at the moment we were at the bottom of a profound trade depression which will sooner or later give way to a period of prosperity. A more candid examination of the facts would probably show us that at the moment we are probably at the height of as great a trade boom as capitalism in Europe is capable of under postwar condtions.

The cause of the rotten distribution of wealth lies in the

nature of the capitalist order of society. Whilst wealth is cooperatively produced, while industries can only be maintained by the co-operative labour of millions of workers, these industries are not owned by the workers who operate them, but by a small idle class owning the land, the banks and the means of production. Because this class owns the means of life, it is able to dictate to the producers the terms on which they will work. These terms may vary for different classes of workers, in accordance with their scarcity, skill, or organisation, but they are always of such a character as to allow to the employing class the lion's share of the wealth which is produced by the labour of others.

In addition to the unequal distribution of wealth, capitalism wastes many of the advantages of science and invention because of the planless character of modern industry taken as a whole. In a single workshop, or even within a single industry, production may be planned according to the most scientific methods, but in capitalist society as a whole there is no plan regulating the production and distribution of wealth. The whole system is based on the pursuit of profit by the owners of the means of production. The regulator of the whole system determining whether industry shall be expanded or shall go on short time is the rise and fall of prices on the market, reflecting the rise and fall in the possibilities of profit for the capitalists whose industries produce for the market.

The planlessness of capitalism taken as a whole renders it incapable of completely utilising the results of modern science and invention or of overcoming the crises in the basic industries in this country. At the present moment it is recognised on all hands that the coal industry in Great Britain is technically in an exceptionally backward state, and even from the standpoint of efficient capitalism, requires to be reorganised from top to bottom. No capitalist will make any effort to reorganise an industry on more efficient lines, however, unless there is the prospects of a vast profit accruing from the expenditure on that reorganisation. As no such return for expenditure on reorganisation is probable in the coal industry at the present moment, the technical backwardness is allowed to remain, while the mine-owners concentrate their attention on cutting wages on the one hand, and forming price rings to extract a higher price from the home consumer of coal on the other hand. The coal industry is left to drift to ruin, while the capitalist class as a whole is diverting its investments into the new luxury industries or into the industries abroad which promise greater profits than the decaying coal industry.

The exact opposite of this is seen in the Socialist industry of Russia, in spite of the meagre resource in a country which is still largely agrarian. The Russian workers have been able in recent years to raise the efficiency of their industry enormously. Should one section of industry in Russia fall behind another section and require assistance from outside, then resources are diverted from the more prosperous industries to the industry which is lagging behind, in order to bring it up to date. The result of this is that the whole of Russian industry is advancing together, no section being neglected and allowed to fall into decay.

The scramble for profit leads also to the scramble for markets for sources of investment and raw materials on an international scale, and leads inevitably to war.

The late war was produced by this scramble for trade and territory, and it has left capitalism in Europe definitely on the downgrade. Even when capitalism was on the upgrade, however, continually expanding year after year, the workers did not receive the advantages of the mighty technical progress that was being made. Many capitalist authorities have argued that the workers, at the end of the nineteenth century, were in a better position than at the beginning of the nineteenth century, as a result of 100 years of capitalist development. It must be pointed out, however, that in relation to the wealth and the luxury enjoyed by the capitalist class, in relation to the capacity of society to produce wealth, the worker was poorer at the end of the nineteenth century than at the beginning. Thus, in the period of the greatest expansion of capitalism, colossal wealth existed alongside the most heartrending poverty.

All this may seem the most elementary Socialism and unworthy of emphasis. The very elements of Socialism, however, are being forgotten by many people in the Labour movement to-day. At the moment the idea is being widely spread that by an improvement in the efficiency of capitalism the workers will be able to obtain a continuous improvement in their standard of life. The Secretary of the Trade Union Congress, Mr. Citrine, writing in the "Manchester Guardian," advocates, for example,

> "that the unions should actively participate in a concerted effort to raise industry to its highest efficiency by developing the most scientific methods of production, eliminating waste and harmful restrictions, removing causes of friction and avoidable conflict and promoting the largest possible output so as to provide a rising standard of life and continuously, improving conditions of employment."

The idea behinds this is that the more capitalism produces wealth the better off everyone will become. This is not the case. The more wealth capitalism produces the greater its difficulties as a functioning system; the more difficult it is to obtain markets, the more intensive international competition becomes; the greater becomes the danger of the antagonisms created by this competition ripening into war. Thus, on the one hand, capitalism, in its development, widens the gulf between the active workers and the non-producing capitalists, increases the difficulties of capitalism to dispose of its product, and drives the capitalist states irresistibly towards war.

The Present Tendency of Capitalism

At the present moment the difficulties of capitalism are increasing in every country in Europe. In the generation previous to the war a great change took place within capitalism. The free competition of individual capitalists competing for the market gave way more and more to the formation of trusts and combines. These trusts and combines commenced to fight each other, not merely by lowering their prices as in the period of free competition, but also by securing to themselves exclusive monopolies of the raw materials of industry. Hence a scramble all over the world for control of oil fields, iron ore deposits and sources of supply of all kinds. The result of this scramble was the war. When the war was over, it was found that capitalism had been shaken to its very foundations. Countries which had formerly been in the very forefront of capitalist "progress" were now almost ruined. New countries which had formerly been dependent upon them, such as Japan and America, had thrown off their dependence and were entering upon a period of expansion. American capitalism particularly attained hitherto unheard-of heights of capitalist prosperity, *but only at the expense of the capitalist countries which were declining, a fact which our Labour leaders and capitalists who ask us to imitate America somewhat conveniently forget.*

Europe particularly, in this period, lost a considerable amount of its former predominance. Its share in world production, trade and commerce declined.

While recently conditions in Europe have somewhat improved as a result of huge American loans, European capitalism has by no means solved the crisis into which the world has plunged it. At the present moment, as was shown by the Economic Conference at Geneva, world production has vastly outrun the seeming power of the world markets, and this is resulting everywhere in an intensification of competition, which European capitalism is finding increasingly difficult to meet.

No country is feeling the effects of these changes more than Great Britain is, because the whole structure of British industry is built on -the assumption of an expanding world market, whereas at the present moment the development of new countries, industrially, is leading to the expansion of production beyond the absorbing powers of the market. Under capitalism this state of affairs naturally leads to intensification of competition, and in no country are the capitalists worse equipped to meet this competition than in Great Britain. The great basic industries of Great Britain on which its former prosperity have been built, iron and steel, shipbuilding, coal mining, the cotton and wool textile industry, have fallen technically behind the industries in the newer countries, which are able to start with the latest methods of production. The consequence is that in these industries a chronic crisis has raged for the past seven years.

This is affecting the international position of Great Britain. In order that a capitalist country is able to function smoothly, it must, in the long run, produce and export capital, consumable goods or services to the value of those which it imports. At the present moment, however, British exports are only 50 per cent. in money values above pre-war, whereas British imports are twice the money value of pre-war. (These figures are from "Principal Features of the World Economic Position" — League of Nations, 1927.) This means that what is called the balance of trade is going against Great Britain, a fact which affects the future of Britain as a capitalist industrial country very much indeed.

In such a situation, the capitalists have only one solution of the difficulty, i.e., the increased exploitation of the working class. There are two ways in which the capitalists can increase this exploitation: (1) to reduce the wages of the working class, and (2) to speed up the working class while continuing to pay them the same wages. These methods are not mutually exclusive. Very often both of them are adopted by the same body of employers, one after the other.

Back to "Normal"

One of the sharpest divisions of opinion existing in the Labour movement to-day is that concerning the attitude which ought to be adopted towards this capitalist attack on the wages and conditions of the working class. The reformist leaders of the Labour movement hold that capitalism, as a result of the war, is not in a "normal" condition. If wage reductions will help in getting capitalism back to "normal," then the majority of the Labour leaders hold that these wage reductions ought to be agreed to by the working class. They have pursued this policy, not merely in theory, but in action when, during the General Strike, the whole weight of the Trade Union leaders was thrown into the endeavour to induce the miners to accept lower wages in order to help capitalism back to "normal." We will see later that this policy of calling upon the workers to make sacrifices in order to help capitalism back to normal, runs through the whole policy of the reformist Labour leaders at the present time.

The Communists contend, on the other hand, that the growing difficulties of the capitalist system are not due to some abnormal accident which has befallen capitalism. The war and the effects of the war are due to the normal development of the capitalist system itself, and no amount of concessions by the workers can do more than meet the immediate difficulties which the capitalist class are faced with. Sooner or later new difficulties will arise in the development of the system, and the capitalists will call upon the workers for further sacrifice. The Communists, therefore, call upon the workers to resist all attempts to lower their standard of life, to unite their forces industrially and to make their resistance as widespread and as united as possible, and having beaten off the capitalist offensive by a united resistance, to come forward from that to an attack on the capitalist system itself. This is one of the fundamental questions dividing the reformist Labour leaders from the Communists. The struggle between the reformists and the Communists is not, as is sometimes pretended, merely a quarrel as to whether force should be used in obtaining the demands of the workers. The dispute between Communists and Labour leaders extends to every aspect of the working class policy. *In the sphere of wages, the reformists stand for concessions to capitalism, in order to help capitalism to get back to "normal," while the Communists stand for a resistance to the demands of the capitalists and the preparation for a decisive struggle against capitalism.*

The reformist policy of concessions to capitalism can be seen in other spheres than that of wage reductions. At the present moment there is passing through the House of Commons an Unemployment Insurance Act which definitely reduces standards of unemployment relief hitherto given to young workers, and which worsens the conditions under which an adult worker can remain on Unemployed Relief. This Bill of the Tory Government, worsening the conditions of the unemployed, is based on the Blanesburgh Report, which was signed by three Labour leaders — Miss Margaret Bondfield, Mr. A. E. Holmes, and Nlr. Frank Hodges. Amongst the large number of contradictory excuses put forward by Miss Bondfield for signing a report which advocated the reduction of the scales of relief of young workers, was the excuse that if the Labour leaders had refrained from signing this report, and had issued a Minority Report of their own, the capitalists would have issued a Majority lkport recommending more drastic cuts in unemployed relief than was done by the Blanesburgh Report, and, therefore, in order to prevent the capitalists recommending too drastic cuts in unemployed relief Miss Bondfield signed the Blanesburgh Report, which advocated some cuts in unemployment relief. Miss Bondfield's policy was not repudiated by the joint conference of Labour Parties and Trade Unions which met to consider the Blanesburgh Report in April, 1927, and was so much in harmony with the general policy of the bureaucracy that she felt genuinely amazed and hurt at the idea that anyone could protest against it.

The Class Struggle in the Present Period

The whole of the present policy of the reformist leaders in the Trade Unions is based on the assumption that capitalism is sooner or later going to get back to a condition of expansion, similar to that which it experienced in pre-war days, and that our first task is therefore to help the capitalists to get the system back to normal and then insist on pushing forward the demand of the workers for higher wages and for better conditions. The Communists declare that the crisis in capitalism is a chronic crisis, that while slight improvements in trade are not impossible, they are extremely unlikely, and if they come about at all they would only be of short duration. The workers cannot, therefore, the Communists maintain, adopt the policy of the Labour leaders, which consists in helping the capitalists to chase after illusory prosperity in the hope that when that prosperity comes the workers may be able to resume their old methods of Trade Union struggle. When the reformists try to excuse their policy by declaring that the workers cannot struggle effectively against the capitalist class in a period of trade depression, the Communists declare that the trade depression is permanent, and the workers must learn how to struggle in this period of trade depression or go down into conditions of barbarism and slavery.

For this struggle against the capitalist offensive in a period of trade depression, the widest possible unity between the employed workers and the unemployed workers is necessary. The whole policy, however, of the leaders of the Trade Union movement is towards the desertion of the unemployed. We have already referred to the case of the signing of the Blanesburgh Report. Another case equally as significant, was the attempt of the General Council of the Trade Union Congress to prevent the miners' march to London, in spite of the fact that the demands of that march were demands which had been endorsed by the whole Labour movement from time to time. In spite of the detailed opposition of the Labour Party to many clauses of the Unemployment Bill, based on the

Blanesburgh Report, that party remains without a definite policy in regard to the unemployed at the present moment. *Thus the one effective way in which the workers can struggle in a period of trade depression, the unity of employed and unemployed, is being sabotaged by the reformist leadership at the present time.*

The same refusal to organise a struggle in accordance with new conditions is observable in Trade Union policy. In spite of the fact that the workers' forces are still hopelessly disorganised between the hundreds of competing unions, the General Council at the last Trade Union Congress brought in a recommendation to the effect that it was impossible to elaborate a plan of Trade Union reorganisation, and that therefore amalgamation and unification of the Trade Union Movement should be left to the initiative of the various unions themselves. This, under present conditions, amounts to a refusal to exercise leadership and to help forward the unification of the working class in the factories and in the industries. In effect, it involves the weakening of the working class in face of the capitalist offensive, which is still continuing.

The refusal of the reformists to create the conditions for a united struggle on the part of the employed and the unemployed against the capitalist offensive, the refusal to use the whole forces of the working class during the General Strike, the betrayal of the General Strike, and the refusal to use the weapon of direct action as a means of combatting the Trade Union Bill, the break with the Russian Unions, have all led to heavy working-class defeats. The miners have been crushed, the Trade Union Bill has been placed on the Statute Book, and now the prediction of the Communists with regard to the attacks on the miners being the preliminary to the attack on other sections of the workers is proved to be correct. At the present moment, the wool textile workers and the cotton textile workers are being threatened with attacks on their wages and conditions of life. In the cotton trades particularly, the forty-eight-hour week, one of the most cherished gains of the working class from their post-war struggles, is being menaced by the employing class. *Yet, in spite of the humiliation that they have suffered at the hands of the capitalist class, in spite of the attacks on the miners and the impending attacks on other workers, in spite of the fact that the Trade Union Bill is on the Statute Book, the Trade Union leaders have no policy except that of appealing to the employing class who have crushed the miners and who propose to crush other sections of the workers, to kindly co-operate with them in a project to realise peace and prosperity on the basis of capitalism.*

Industrial Peace

One can hardly understand the mental processes of individuals who as Trade Union negotiators have been unable to persuade the capitalists to refrain from attacking the wages of the workers, but now, after a series of such attacks, are entertaining (or, worse still, pretending to entertain) the fond delusion that by getting together with the same wage-cutting employers in an "industrial peace" conference they will not only be able to create a regime of industrial prosperity but will be able to win higher wages for the workers without the necessity of a large-scale industrial struggle.

The whole idea underlying this "industrial peace" stunt is well expressed by Mr. William Straker, the Secretary of the Northumberland Miners' Association. Mr. Straker is the miners' leader in a district where wages have been cut to the barest possible minimum compatible with existence and where terror and victimisation have been systematically applied by the employers against the workers.

The brutal attacks of the employing class have not engendered in Mr. Straker a spirit of resistance, but, on the contrary, have filled him with the milk of human kindness.

In his monthly circular to the members of the Northumberland Miners' Association, Mr. Straker, welcoming the new "Industrial Peace" Conference, says, "So I welcome any movement which has for its object the bringing of men

37

representing different interests in the industrial world together for the purpose of hearing each other's views on what is the best thing to be done in order to restore industrial prosperity." One would imagine that Mr. Straker had heard the mine-owners' views on that question often enough both in the lock-out of 1921 and the lock-out of 1926. We must welcome, however, Mr. Straker's naive argument for the "industrial peace" conference. The capitalist management of industry, it appears, has not created prosperity, but if a few Trade Union leaders meet a group of leading capitalists, then, according to Mr. Straker, they will be able to talk things over, and as a result of this talk, prosperity will be won for the industry without the vested interests of the capitalists being affected in any way. It is a pity that Mr. Straker did not expose his ideas to, the mine-owners during the two lock-outs which we have just named. They would doubtless have been pleased to know how to restore the industry to prosperity without reducing wages and without giving up any of their claims on the profits of that industry.

It is quite clear from what we have quoted from Mr. Citrine in another part of this pamphlet, that the whole policy of "industrial peace" is based on the capitalist rationalisation of industry. In the speeches of the advocates of "industrial peace" we are told about the backward condition of British industry, how it is not trustified on as great a scale as the industries in other countries which are competing with us; how it neglects to utilise the latest machinery and the latest methods of securing a full output from the workers, such as the running band associated with the name of Henry Ford, and the stop-watch associated with Taylor, and the other scientific management experts.

We are told by the advocates of rationalisation and "industrial peace" that surely no intelligent person can object to the scientific rationalisation of industry resulting in a greater output per man. We have got to remember, however, that we are living in capitalist society, and when we talk about rationalisation under capitalism, we have got to ask ourselves who is carrying through this rationalisation, and in whose interests is the rationalisation conceived. If the capitalist class is left in control of industry and carry through the rationalisation on their own lines, then obviously such rationalisation will serve the interests of the exploiting class and not the interests of the workers.

This can be seen more clearly if we examine the phrase "co-operation between the Trade Unions and the capitalist class." As we have seen in the earlier part of this pamphlet, the workers are co-operating in industry to produce wages for themselves and profits for the capitalists. Every day the worker co-operates in the workshop with the representatives of capitalist management. In what way can the Trade Unions (under capitalism) make this co-operation more effective in producing wealth than it is at the present time? *In one way alone*. The workers have, in the course of a long struggle to obtain a decent standard of life under capitalism, built up certain customs and rules which they endeavour to apply in the workshop. Certain classes of work are the monopoly of certain classes of workers, and the capitalists, in the union shops, must employ those workers on the job and no others. Certain trades having had long experience of piece work and of the habit of the employers of cutting piece prices, place definite restrictions on piece work, and in some cases oppose it altogether. Other bodies of workers, knowing the effects of the introduction of new machinery on their standard of life, try to get prior consultation with the employers before the new machine is introduced so that the terms on which the new machine is operated will be such as will maintain their accustomed standard of life. All those Trade Union restrictions and customs, built up to defend the workers' standards against an hostile class, are, to a certain extent, barriers against the most intensive utilisation of equipment and labour power by the capitalists, and the capitalists, particularly in the engineering trades, have always tried to break them down. The only way in which Trade Union leaders can cooperate with the capitalists is restoring "prosperity" (i.e., increasing production) is to induce the workers to forgo their customs and restrictions, allow the capitalists a freer hand in utilising the labour-power which is available to them in order that an increased product may result. The Trade Union leaders will, of course, point out to the capitalists, as they have done in Germany, that this increased production requires to be marketed, and that the employers ought to ensure a stable home market by increasing the workers' wages as fast, if not faster, than the increased production. They forget the employing class is anxious to introduce those new methods because of a desire for a greater profit, and is not concerned with ensuring a market for his goods through the increase of wages and the reduction of his own profits, and therefore he looks not to a home market made prosperous by the increase in workers' wages, but to the foreign market where he can rely on a maximum possible profit.

It must further be realised that this policy of rationalisation is bound, if widely applied, to increase the unemployed army enormously, so that when the division of the increased production comes up for consideration, the workers will be hampered in their efforts to get a share of it by the mass of the unemployed existing outside the factory gates and by the persistent refusal of the Trade Union leaders too organise the unemployed alongside, the employed.

Thus, even if the workers were to agree to facilitate production by abandoning their safeguards, there is no guarantee that they would get a share of the increased production. The division of the increased product would be settled like the division of the product to-day, by the relative economic strength of the workers on the one hand and the employers on the other. Thus, the "industrial peace" proposals for rationalisation, whilst offering the capitalists the certainty of increased profits, hold out no hopes to the workers at all.

The idea that by so improving production the capitalist class, can overcome the crisis which they are in, is stupid. Great

Britain is not the only country where the capitalists are proposing to rationalise industry. All capitalist countries are engaged in the same work. The only result of this rationalisation under capitalism is a growing crisis in the world market, a growing scramble for colonies and for markets, and the bringing nearer of a new world war. Thus the Trade Union leaders who are leading the workers to believe that a far-reaching improvement in the workers' wages and conditions of life can be got not by overthrowing capitalism, but by co-operating with the capitalists to make their system more efficient, are simply surrendering to the capitalist class, misleading the workers, and creating conditions which will inevitably make the rich richer and the workers poorer.

The Struggle for Power

The economic struggle against the capitalist offensive inevitably raises the question of political power, because in every large-scale struggle the capitalist class mobilises all the forces of the capitalist state against the working class. They have placed on the Statute Book the Emergency Powers Act, which suspends all Constitutional guarantees during a state of emergency, and gives the Government of the day power to do anything it pleases with the Labour movement. They have further placed on the Statute Book the Trade Union Act, which prevents the workers in one industry coming to the assistance, with industrial action or with finance, of the workers of another industry engaged in a trade dispute, though no law which could possibly be framed would be effective in preventing the capitalists of one industry from helping the capitalists in another industry during such a dispute.

The more the workers unite their forces and commence to struggle against the capitalist offensive, the more the struggle becomes a political struggle, not between the workers and any group of capitalists, but between the workers and the capitalist state representing the capitalist class as a whole. Every section of the Labour movement, therefore, believes in the necessity for capturing political power.

The present Labour leadership preaches occasionally that political power can be captured by securing a Parliamentary majority, and this Parliamentary majority will enable the workers to transform society from capitalism to Socialism in a peaceful, painless fashion. We sometimes hear the supporters of this point of view declaring "I do not believe in the physical force methods advocated by the Communists. I believe that we can get all that we want through the medium of Parliament." The workers have to remember, however, that what we are faced with is not a question of belief, but a question of fact. Are the facts which we see unfolding themselves before our eyes every day of such a character as to induce us to believe in the possibility of a peaceful democratic transformation of capitalism?

It has long been the contention of the Communists that underneath the democratic pretence of Parliament the actual political power of the country is in the hands of the small capitalist class who direct policy in their own interests. So long as this small capitalist class is able, by using its economic power, the control of the Press and of the sources of information, to secure a democratic majority in Parliament or in local government agreeing with this point of view, it loudly proclaims its belief in democracy. If, however, the democratic vote should begin to go against the interests of the capitalist class, it will not hesitate to smash the democratic pretence and establish an open dictatorship. We see the proof of that to-day in local government. The Boards of Guardians in this country were appointed by law to look after the interests of the poor. So long as those Boards were in capitalist hands and the poor, whether infirm or able-bodied, were treated with the utmost callousness and contempt, those Boards of Guardians were allowed to continue their democratic ways undisturbed. Immediately, however, Labour majorities began to appear on those Boards and began to utilise them in the interests of the working class, the capitalist government immediately restricted their powers through their Board of Guardians Default Act, and in cases where the Guardians were recalcitrant, superseded them by nominated commissions. Exactly the same thing applies to local municipal bodies, which are now prevented from utilising their powers in certain directions by the Local Authorities Audit Bill.

The same process is taking place in Parliament itself. At the very moment when the Trade Union leaders were telling the working class to wait till the next election and use their votes in order to repeal the Trade Union Act, the Tory Government was considering a scheme of House of Lords reform which would enable the reactionaries of this country to practically bring to a standstill the work of any Labour Government seriously intent on improving the condition of the working class or of removing the restrictions, such as the Trade Union Act, which the Tory Government has recently placed on the Labour movement.

Even if these barriers were broken down, however, there are still other barriers to be overcome by the Parliamentary Labour majority seriously intent on fighting for the working class. The bureaucracy in our State Departments, the key posts in the Army and Navy, are held by the big men of the capitalist class. These people would not permit the gradual elimination of capitalism from our social life. They would resist and sabotage, and would be supported by the immense financial resources at the disposal of the capitalist class. A Labour Government reahy intent on fighting for the worker would therefore either have to call on the working class to break this resistance by direct action and proceed to transform itself from a Parliamentary Government to a Government resting on the organisations of the working class, or it would have to abandon the struggle against capitalism.

When people talk about the Communists advocating bloodshed they have got to realise that all indications go to show that the present possessing class will defend itself by force, and the people who are asking for bloodshed are not the

Communists, who point out this fact to the working class, but those who tell the workers that they can get everything by the vote. If the capitalist class is going to resist the workers, then their resistance is likely to be of short duration if the workers are prepared beforehand, if they are thoroughly organised in industry, if a resolute Communist Party has carried out a propaganda in the Army and the Navy. on the other hand, if none of these things is done, then not only is bloodshed certain, but the defeat of the working class in consequence of this bloodshed is, also extremely likely.

There is, however, another body of opinion which says to the Communists, "We agree that the capitalist class will resist by force, but if this is so, surely at any rate it is desirable for the workers to get a Parliamentary majority behind them before attempting to forcibly overthrow the capitalist class. Is it not a fact," they say, "that much of Cromwell's success in the struggle against the monarchy was due to the fact that he had Parliament behind him?" We have got to remember, however, the difference between the capitalist revolution and the workers' revolution. The capitalist class grew up within the framework of pre-capitalist society and became an economically powerful class without any revolution. Their revolution was designed to secure for them such political control as would enable them to break down all restrictions and secure the fullest possible development for their industry and trade which they already controlled. With them economic power preceded political power. The workers, on the other hand, cannot get economic power without first, by a political revolution, breaking down the capitalist state machine, building up their political power in the form of a workers' state, and on that basis proceeding to secure control of the economic forces of society.

The question of whether the workers should attempt to seize power before or after obtaining a Parliamentary majority is entirely a question of time, place, and circumstance. The workers are engaged in a struggle with the capitalist class and cannot determine their policy without reference to the policy of

44

their capitalist adversaries. Capitalist society is continually creating crises in the course of its development, such as the revolutionary crisis which seized all Europe in its grip at the end of the world war. It is the duty of Communists to prepare the workers to utilise such crises for the overthrow of the capitalists, whether the workers have a Parliamentary majority or not.

Good-bye, Socialism!

The immediate situation we are faced with in Great Britain, however, is not that the capitalist class will resist the Labour Government seriously intent on achieving Socialism, but that the next Labour Government will make no serious attempt to achieve Socialism at all. Since the experience of 1924 Labour Government, the dominant leadership of the Labour movement had been working gradually to weaken and modify the already very weak and moderate reformist programme formulated by the Labour Party in 1915. The capital levy which was advocated by Labour in the three General Elections has now been dropped in favour of a proposal called the surtax. This is how Mr. MacDonald explains why the capital levy was dropped: —

> "Some years ago we proposed a capital levy. It was, not an income tax, and was not in the nature of an income tax. It was a call upon capital, and no one who knew anything about economics would have suggested that the revenue from such a call could have been used for anything except paying off of the national debt. We wished to reduce the national debt for reasons which were theoretically sound and industrially advantageous, *but the country did not allow us to proceed*. The levy was the most businesslike way out, not the only way, and so we adopted another."

Nothing can be more false than the suggestion that the country, that is to say, the mass of the electorate, did not allow the Labour Party to proceed. The capital levy was a popular part of Labour's programme, and at each successive election when it was brought forward increasing votes were registered for the Labour Party. The capital levy was dropped not because of the opposition of the country, but because of the opposition of the big banks, a fact tacitly acknowledged in the Labour Minority Report of the Colwyn Committee, which considered the question of the capital levy. In spite of all talk about the surtax, no substitute for the capital levy has been adopted by the Labour Party. *The surtax is simply a tax on unearned income, and that was already a part of Labour's programme at the moment when the capital levy was advocated.*

In its Blackpool resolution on Unemployment, the Labour Party has deliberately eliminated even the suggestion of Socialist proposals which were incorporated in the resolutions of previous conferences, and has watered down its policy to a few vague phrases.

With regard to the nationalisation of the mines, while the policy of nationalisation is retained as a pious aspiration, a resolution was passed at Blackpool which will give the Labour Government an opportunity and excuse for introducing not nationalisation, but unification and trustification on the lines of the Samuel Memorandum. More and more Labour Party policy is being adapted to the needs of capitalism.

The conflict between the Communists and the reformists leadership of the Labour movement is not merely a conflict between one body which believes that force may have to be utilised for a realisation of Socialism, and another body which believes force is unnecessary for this purpose. *It is becoming increasingly a conflict between the Communists standing for a Socialist working-class policy and the reformist leadership who have neither hope nor desire to realise Socialism peacefully or in any other way, but are bent on adapting all Labour policy to*

46

the necessities of capitalism.

Reformism in Foreign Policy

Nowhere is this rapprochement of the Labour Party to the capitalist parties more apparent or more dangerous than in the sphere of foreign policy. This can be seen in the attitude towards the Tory Government break with Soviet Russia.

Every impartial person on the Continent of Europe recognises the fact of the persistent hostility of the British Tory Government to Soviet Russia, and of its repeated attempts to form a European bloc against Soviet Russia. In breaking with Russia, Sir Austen Chamberlain clearly showed himself to be the aggressor. In spite of his talk about the impossibility of maintaining normal diplomatic intercourse with Russia we have the fact that most other capitalist states are able to maintain this intercourse. The break with Russia was preceded in Great Britain by an intense campaign preparing the way for the break. In this campaign, the great oil interests, being competed out of their high profits by the Socialist oil industry of Russia, took the lead, and with them were united all the capitalist elements who feared Russian influence in China, and amongst the oppressed peoples generally. The Labour leadership made a feeble and half-hearted protest in Parliament against the Tory diplomatic break with Russia, but immediately after proceeded to help the Government by protesting against the execution of twenty "White" conspirators for counter-revolutionary activity in Russia. The Labour resolution which was passed condemning those executions led it to be inferred that the executions were not for counter-revolutionary activity, but were a mere act of revenge for the assassination of the Soviet Ambassador in Poland. This lie was even defended at the Labour Party Conference, when Geo. Lansbury said:

> "That the reason he supported, and the Executive supported, this resolution was, first of all, because the

Russian Soviet authorities themselves issued a statement that these men were executed owing to the murder of the Russian Ambassador to Poland. (Dissent.) Yes, and he was prepared to supply any comrade, if he would write to Eccleston Square, with the authority for the statement he had just made, and that they were being executed in order to stop the terrorism that was arising abroad and in Russia itself. That was the first ground. The next ground was that the Labour movement of this country, ever since he had known it — and he had known it a number of years, long before the Party was started in this country — had always stood against execution for political offences."

There is no truth whatever in the statement that these men were executed for revenge, and not because of their counterrevolutionary activity. Yet when this is called attention to at the Labour Party Conference, the Chairman of the Labour Party repeats the lie, and adds to it the lie that the Labour Party has always been against execution for political offences. The Labour Party did not fight against the execution of James Conolly or Sir Roger Casement for political offences during the war.

Further propaganda against the Soviet Union was emitted at the same Congress, when Mr. MacDonald said: —

"He would say to those who were always talking about defending Russia, that the most effective way of defending Russia was not to give Russia excuses for having a wrong international policy. They were told that Russia had done this, that, and the other thing. It was not true. Russia had taken no effective steps whatever to get into relationship of neighbourly union with the other States of Europe. Again and again that question had been raised, and it had been pressed upon the Russian Government, but no satisfactory answer had been given. Until the Russian Government made its relations perfectly clear with the Third International, that desirable step could never be taken. It was no use talking nonsense about it. They knew perfectly well that every time a move was made to get an understanding with Russia it was upset by the political propaganda of an organisation which was destroying goodwill towards Russia on the part of millions of people who really desired to show their goodwill."

Here we have an attempt to put the blame on to Russia for the international situation at the present day, and the implication that after all, that if Chamberlain has made some mistakes, the Russians have to a great extent provoked him by their unwise policy. This anti-Russian attitude, which is an obsession with Mr. MacDonald, was further developed in the article in "Forward." Referring to the Russian offer of disarmament at the League of Nations, Mr. MacDonald could scarcely avoid sneering at the proposals which were rousing the enthusiasm of the workers everywhere. He said: —

"Meanwhile, the Russians have thrown their bomb shell into the midst of the Disarmament Commission. It is big and comprehensive. It belonged to the type of 'the whole hog.' But, will it burst? Or, is it only a Christmas cracker with its finger at its nose? Whatever it is, it is there in the offices of Geneva, and will have to be taken into account, and when it is being examined I hope the Russians will be present to give some detailed information about it. It certainly begins at the wrong end, and may only result in prolonging what has already become a criminal waste of time. If the Russian method is the right one, then God made the world, and especially man, all wrong, for there is not a nation, except a few small ones, that will pursue it. Some of my friends want examples of nations throwing away their arms, and I shall do everything I can to help them. *May one, therefore, appeal to Russia, as it has set down such a high standard on paper, to proceed to carry it out in practice, whatever happens at Geneva. I fear that nothing of the kind will happen.*"

In other words, Mr. MacDonald is suggesting in the last sentence that if the Russians do not agree to completely disarm themselves before a hostile capitalist world, after that capitalist world has rejected their proposals, then those proposals for simultaneous disarmament were absolutely insincere.

An even more glaring example of Labour Party support of Conservative foreign policy is to be found in the recent Labour Party attitude towards the Indian Commission. Every schoolboy knows that Great Britain entered India not to civilise the Indian people but to seize the country by force of arms with a view to increasing the profits of British capitalists. In fact, during one half of its existence under British rule, India was governed not directly by the British Government but through the medium of a trading company, the East India Company. Our motive in entering India was profit; our justification for remaining in India is the sword.

Recently the Tory Government appointed under the Government of India Act, 1919, a Commission to go to India to inquire to what extent the Indians were fitted for a measure of self-government. To anyone who is capable of getting outside of the Imperialist prejudice created by the capitalist class, such a Commission was an insult to India. Here is a Government, unable to solve its own unemployment problem, unable to solve its housing problem, unable to prevent unnecessary infantile mortality, unable to create: the conditions of a civilised life for the majority of the people in Great Britain, sending a

Commission to India to discover whether the Indians are fit for self-government.

The whole basis of this Commission lies in its responsibility to the British Parliament. In the last analysis it is the Parliament of the Imperialist conquerors which is to decide how far India was fit for self-government.

The Labour Party knew that such a Commission was going to be appointed, and at the Blackpool Conference they passed a resolution affirming the right of the Indian people "to full self-government and self-determination" and declaring "that the Commission to be appointed under the Government of India Act should be so constituted, and in the method of doing its work so arranged, that it will enjoy the confidence and co-operation of the Indian people." Immediately the composition and scope of the Commission became known in India it was plain that the Commission would not evoke the confidence and co-operation of the Indian people. In spite of this fact, the Labour Party supported the Tory Government against the protests of the Indian people and allowed its members to go on the Commission. Mr. Hartshorn, a representative (?) of the miners who were so brutally treated by Birkenhead's Government last year, becomes the agent of Lord Birkenhead in maintaining the enslavement of the Indian people. It is true that the Labour Party declared that they were in favour of an Indian Commission being set up alongside the Commission composed of Britishers and have declared that they will fight for the report of this Commission to be accepted by the British Parliament.

In any case, however, the arbiter of the destinies of the Indian people, the body which will discuss the Commission's reports, will be the British Parliament. In other wards, the Labour Party has reduced self-determination for India to mean the right of the Indians to make a report to the British Parliament, which that Parliament can accept or reject.

The Labour Party has striven desperately to explain its position, but nothing can conceal the fact that it supported the

Tory Government against the Indian people and that while it is suggesting that the Tory plan should be modified by the appointment of an Indian Commission alongside the British one, it is the Tory plan and not the Labour Party's which is operative to-day. In any case, the Labour Party's plan is merely the Tory plan camouflaged in order to mislead the Indian people.

Thus the Labour Party, which begins by co-operating with the capitalists on the home front in order to bring capitalism back to normal, co-operates with capitalism in foreign policy. Such co-operation in times of peace is the prelude to co-operation with capitalism in times of war.

The Communist Party, on the other hand, declares that the Indian people fighting for independence, are fighting the same enemy as the British working class here at home and that therefore the British working class must form. a united front with them in the struggle to overthrow British Imperialism. The present policy of the Labour Party is therefore leading away from Socialism towards the rebuilding of capitalism, towards the intensified enslavement of the colonial peoples and towards war.

What Can be Done

In these circumstances, if the British working-class desire to beat off the capitalist attacks on their present standards, avoid the danger of war and carry out a resolute struggle to achieve their emancipation through the overflow of capitalism, they must fight more and more within the Labour movement against the reformist policy of co-operating with capitalism.

The necessary preliminary to carrying on an effective fight against the Reformist corruption of the Labour movement is the building up of a strong Communist Party. Unless the active workers who see the. dangers of this reformist policy get together and build up a revolutionary Communist Party their influence in the Labour Movement will be reduced to nothing by the weight of the reformist machine in the Trade Unions and in the Labour Party which is in the hands of men who are deterrkined on co-operation with capitalism at any price.

The Communist Party is alone equipped to fight reformism, the bulwark of capitalism in the Labour Movement, because the Communist Party alone has an alternative outlook and policy to that of the reformists. Its views as to the tendencies of capitalist society, its predictions as to the development of the struggle between Capital and Labout in Great Britain, have been borne out by the events of recent months. The Communist Party is therefore equipped to guide the working class in the struggle. It is not afraid to tell the working class unpopular truths or to risk temporary misunderstanding. It knows that the experience of the working class in the struggle will more and more convince them of the correctness of Communist policy.

Only such a political party can aid the workers in reorganising the Trade Union Movement on more efficient and scientific lines. The old leadership of the Trade Unions wedded to obsolete methods, fighting in defence of vested interests, must be eliminated and replaced by a new leadership pursuing a new policy. Such a policy would be based on the freest possible democracy within the Unions and the elimination of all forms of administrative waste which are common in a number of Unions at the present time. It would pursue the task of welding together the scattered Unions of the present day into powerful industrial Unions, linked up under a General Council of the T.U.C., cleansed from faint hearts and traitors. It would organise the unemployed and bring the unemployed organisation into close permanent association with the Trade Union Movement on a common policy. Above all, in view of the drift towards the rationalisation of industry, it would seek to develop powerful factory committees which can, backed by the Trade Union Movement, fight against such forms of capitalist rationalisation as are calculated to reduce the standard of life of the works, and from that, build up the strength of the workers in the factories for the struggle for the overthrow of capitalism.

Within the Labour Party, the members of the Communist Party will work with all progressive left-wing workers in fighting against the capitalist policy of the Labour leadership for a Socialist policy, not only by putting forward on every possible occasion, an alternative left-wing policy to that of the Labour leaders, but in struggling for a change in leadership of the Labour Party and also a change in the personnel of the House of Commons, changing those M.P.'s who have ceased to express the workers' point of view, for those who are prepared to act in the House of Commons as the spokesmen of the struggling masses outside. The Communist Party will, of course, maintain its independent struggle as a Communist Party endeavouring through elections to create a powerful Communist group in the House of Commons expressing the mass struggle outside the House and acting as a spur to the left-wing within the Labour Party.

Whilst pursuing this policy, the Communist Party will help a Labour Government into office, not because it believes that a Labour Government composed of the present leadership will emancipate the workers, but because it believes that such a Government will expose to the working class the futility of reformism and Parliamentarianism and compel them to go forward to the complete overthrow of the capitalist class.

The development of the Communist Party means, therefore, not merely the ultimate victory of the working class, but means success as opposed to surrender in the daily struggle of the workers. All workers who are tired of the half-heartedness and compromise of the Labour leaders, their desertion of Socialism, their co-operation with the capitalist class, should join the Communist Party and help forward the struggle for complete working class emancipation.

Trade Unions and the General Election

ALL active trade unionists are familiar with reactionary managers who are not afraid to declare their intention of wresting from the workers their war-time gains. "Don't think we will give you these piece-rates after the war." "We won't tolerate interference from the shop stewards after the war is over." How often have trade unionists listened to thinly concealed threats of this type. If, at the next General Election, a Government which reflected the views of these reactionary employers and managements wins a majority of votes, the trade union movement would be confronted with a dangerous and difficult situation.

POST-WAR WAGES

Take the vexed question of wages. The official figures in the last Budget White Paper show that prices have advanced by more than 54 per cent.

Only in two industries—mining and agriculture—where wage rates were exceptionally low before the war, have the increases in wage rates kept pace with the rising prices.

In industries like engineering, shipbuilding and docks, the advance in wage-rates lags far behind the increased prices. At the same time, there has been a leap in productivity of over 30 per cent. during the war, and profits have increased by 84 per cent.

So the workers are producing more and are having to pay more for the things they need.

How do the workers manage to meet these increased prices and pay the increased taxes?

In some industries, by working a great deal of overtime.

But in a group of industries like printing, public utilities, transport, food and railways, most of the workers have not been able to increase their earnings by overtime. Their real earnings are far below the pre-war level.

Thus, as excessive overtime ceases, the bulk of the working class will find themselves earning much lower real wages (wages measured by what they can buy) than was the case before the war.

It is an absolute certainty that the unions will proceed immediately the war is over to insist on an all-round increase in wages. Will the Government help or hinder them?

DIRECTION OF JOBS

Or take the question of directing workers to a job. The Minister of Labour hopes that most workers will voluntarily return to their peace-time occupations. But suppose there are not sufficient workers offering their services to vital industries? The Minister will have power to direct workers to them. If we have a Minister of Labour in a progressive Government, he would not set out to direct Labour, but would attract workers to priority jobs by compelling employers to give better pay and conditions. Whereas a Tory Minister of Labour would want to use compulsion in directing workers back to low-paid but vital industries, as for example cotton weaving.

Many of the women who have replaced men during the war have received wages approximating the men's rates. Are they now to be forced back to the ill-paid, unorganised occupations which they were in previously? The Minister has promised that all poorly organised industries shall be covered by Wages Councils which will fix wages and conditions. A sympathetic Government will expedite the formation of such Councils. A Tory Government will sabotage them.

WAR-TIME GAINS

To what extent are we to retain in the post-war years

those war-time innovations that are of value to the workers? There is, for example, the right which the worker now has to appeal against arbitrary dismissals. This is an important check on the arbitrary tyranny of managers and foremen. It ought to be retained in a new form after the war.

In a whole series of industries the workers have received the guaranteed week. The employer cannot give them a job on Monday and Tuesday and send them home on Wednesday because he has no work for them. He must pay for their full week's wages. Such a measure ensures greater stability of wages for the workers, and will force the employers to organise their industries in a more intelligent fashion. The employers are hostile to this measure. In one of the B.B.C. talks on Full Employment, Mr. Walker, a textile employer, explained that he wanted to be in a position to accept an order which would provide work for two days and engage workers to work on it without having any obligations to them, after the two days' work was completed. A Tory Government dominated by the big employers would allow this; but a progressive Government would insist on the guarauteed week.

FACTORY COMMITTEES

Then there is the whole question of the future of the trade union workshop organisation—the shop stewards committees and similar organisations. A large section of the employers are hostile to them. They want to end collective bargaining on piece-work and similar questions in the workshop and go back to the bad old system when prices or times for the job were decided by "mutual agreement" between the workmen and the rate fixer, with the firm's unconditional right to sack held in the background.

Of course, the more far-seeing managements will not refuse to recognise the unions. They will simply ensure that the more militant shop stewards shall have a short life inside their particular factory.

Doubtless the Trade Union movement will do its very best to protect the shop stewards but why should they not be protected by law as is the case in France to-day, where a progressive Government is in power?

Recently the French Provisional Government passed a law establishing Factory Committees (*Comités d'Entreprise*) in all establishments whether industrial, commercial or distributive, employing more than 100 workers.

The works representatives are elected from a panel chosen by the trade unions. They cannot be dismissed by the employer on any pretext without the consent of the Ministry of Labour.

These Factory Committees are entrusted with the management of factory welfare institutions, canteens and day nurseries.

They have the right to advise the management on all production questions. If the Committees are dissatisfied with the management's reply they have the right to appeal to the Minister of Labour.

The Committees have also the right to be informed of the firm's financial position and its production programme.

The firm's balance sheet must be submitted to the Committee before going to the shareholders. Would it not be well worth while to support the shop stewards' committees in Britain by similar legislation?

The strengthening of all forms of workshop organisation is also necessary so that the work of the Joint Production Committees can be maintained and developed, or, in cases where Joint Production Committees do not exist as yet, they can be set up.

In the new proposals for the post-war regulation of wages the Minister of Labour proposes to take powers to compel all employers to observe the trade union rate of wages for the district. More than this is surely necessary. There are quite a number of firms which categorically refuse to negotiate with trade unions representing the workers. Is it not time that this minority of firms were compelled by law to recognise trade unions, and so grant to their workers the right of collective bargaining? No Tory Government is likely to coerce employers for this purpose. But a progressive Government would take a strong line with them.

JOBS FOR ALL

Next to conditions of work the trade unionist wants a steady job. Full employment is said to be the aim of all Parties. It would be a mistake, however, to imagine that the average employer wants a permanent state of full employment where there are more jobs than men. Naturally no employer wants chronic mass unemployment on the scale that existed between the wars. But reactionary employers have no objection to some unemployment, for this reinforces the threat to sack, and helps the employers to maintain "discipline" and keep wages low. Full employment can only be based on a great social programme and policy of raising conditions here and abroad. There will undoubtedly be a great deal of employing class opposition to the practical measures which are necessary to carry out such sweeping reforms, for these involve control of prices and supplies, preventing monopoly cashing-in on the people's needs, taking over the land for housing, and so on. The general control of the economic system by the State, which full employment entails, will be greatly strengthened if vital industries like steel, fuel and power and transport are brought under public ownership. Quite a number of employers who want a high level of employment will be in violent opposition to the measures which are necessary to achieve it. So unless a progressive Government is in power full employment may prove to be as empty a slogan as homes for heroes was at the end of the last war.

PEOPLE'S PEACE

The unions are not merely concerned with wages and conditions but with the successful conclusion of the war against Fascism. They want the punishment of the Fascist war criminals and all the necessary measures taken to make sure that neither Germany, Japan, nor any other country will ever again be able to bring war into the world.

They are determined to see this war through to victory over Fascism, no matter what the cost, or how bitter the sacrifices still to come, or the demands for production still to be made. They want to be sure that this is the last war.

Lasting peace will make it possible for the nations to co-operate for trade. It will help to reduce that international trade war and cut-throat competition which leads to armed war. International co-operation between the United Nations would mean that Britain would be prosperous, that we could assist in the restoration of devastated Europe and help the industrial and social development of a free India and of other Colonial countries, in common with other nations.

All this would mean that British industry would be called on to supply large quantities of goods to these countries, especially engineering products, and that in return we would receive goods which we need. The amount of work would be increased, wages could rise, there would be real town and country planning, more leisure for all kinds of sport, cultural and educational development.

A Britain and a world like this would be possible provided that, after the war, the nations co-operate with each other for maintaining peace and in the use of the world's resources.

What does this mean, practically? In Europe, the nations with whom we shall have to be on good terms and with whose Governments ours will have to co-operate, will, in most cases, have democratic and progressive governments. The Soviet

Union, with whom our 20 years' Alliance is a cornerstone of peace and international co-operation, has a Socialist Government.

A Tory Government, representing Big Business, would try to weaken the Peoples' Governments of Europe. What has happened over Greece shows this. It would be more inclined to compete, as in the pre-war years, with America; and its relations with the Socialist Soviet Union could never be really secure.

These are among the reasons why trade unionists desire that the trade unions are represented at the Peace Conference: a demand on the agenda of the World Trade Union Conference which meets in February. Trade unionists realise the responsibility of their organisations to secure international co-operation and to prevent attempts from Britain or America to install reactionary regimes in Europe or to undermine the Peoples' Governments which already exist.

A Tory Government, after the General Election would make these aims of trade unionists infinitely harder to achieve; but a Progressive Government would lead the way towards international co-operation and the building of a secure and lasting peace.

Now all these questions, to which we could add many more, are of immediate importance. The trade unions do not advocate them as items in a programme to be realised in the distant future. They must be realised in the first months of the post-war years if the workers' conditions are to be safeguarded.

The unions therefore want the post-war General Election to throw up a Government which will carry out the measures needed to realise these immediate aspirations.

THE TORIES' CARDS

Now to defeat the Tories and get such a Government will not be easy. The Tories have strong cards to play. The war with Japan will still be on and the argument will be used that

Churchill, who led us to victory in Europe, must remain to lead us to victory in the Far East.

The Tories will appeal to the country on what looks to be a quite progressive programme. A National Health Service, a comprehensive system of Social Insurance and a great housing programme will be amongst measures they promise. Indeed, they will promise many of the same reforms as the Labour Party does.

But the people must remember that the Tory Party is not in the main composed of earnest social reformers, but of hard-headed business men who will not hesitate to repudiate their promises and even get rid of Churchill if it suits them after the Election is over.

In order to defeat the Tories there will have to be many progressive victories in town and country constituencies that are traditionally Tory strongholds.

This in our opinion can only be achieved if the progressive forces of the country are united, behind a common programme. If the Tories relying on the personal prestige of Churchill are confronted with a competent team of leaders with a wide popular appeal backed by all progressive organisations, they will be decisively defeated.

The unity of the progressive forces to break Tory domination was represented at the last Labour Party Conference as a trick on the part of the Communist and Common Wealth Parties to coerce the Labour Party into giving them seats at the next General Election. This imputation is suspicion mania. The object of progressive unity is not to divide seats which the Labour Party would win in any case. It is to unite all progressives in a powerful united campaign to win seats which in the absence of unity could not be won.

The Labour Party will have to put up the greatest political campaign in all its history. It will have to win every possible ally. It has the responsibility of bringing all working-class and progressive organisations together so that an agreement can be reached regarding electoral unity against the Tories. To rely, as some Labour Party spokesmen indicate, on a political swing of new voters to its support, is to play a dangerous game. It is like a poorly organised trade union deciding on a strike, and hoping that the mass of non-unionists would follow it. In short, it is an exceedingly hazardous gamble.

The proposal for progressive unity relies on a powerful coordinated campaign of the progressive forces, in which every politically active person is mobilised to bring about that gigantic turnover in votes that is necessary if victory is to be secured.

Many people will doubt the possibility of the Labour Party acting on its own defeating the Tories. They will have no doubt whatever of victory over the Tories if they see the progressive forces united behind a single candidate in each constituency.

What are the arguments against the policy? They are summarised in *Man and Metal*, the journal of the Iron and Steel Trades Confederation, in its December issue:

"The constitution of the Labour Party, in the provision it makes for individual membership, when anyone who accepts its constitution can join and have ample scope to work for the achievement of the Party's aims, is such that there is no organic need for making any arrangements for seeking accommodation with other separate political bodies."

Alas, the writer is concealing from his readers the fact that the constitution of the Labour Party provides membership not only for individual membership but affiliated membership. The constitution states

"Affiliated members shall consist of Trade Unions affiliated to the Trades Union Congress or recognised by the General Council of the Trades Union Congress as bona-fide Trade Unions, (*b*) Co-operative Societies and (*c*) Socialist Societies."

Now, the Communist Party has always been prepared to affiliate to the Labour Party on the same terms as is the Fabian Society at present. It would accept Labour Party discipline and act as a unit of the Labour Party in the same way as the Iron and Steel Confederation does. This proposal for unity was put forward at the Labour Party Conference in 1943 and turned down.

So when Labour Party members say to the Communist Party "Come into the Labour Party" the Communists' answer is perfectly clear: "We are willing to come in on the same terms as the Iron and Steel Trades Confederation or any other trade union, or the Fabian Society."

The writer in *Man and Metal* conceals from his readers that the Communist Party has offered to affiliate to the Labour Party and suggests that the Communist Party should dissolve and its members should join the Labour Party as individuals.

But the members of his own trade union are equally free to join the Labour Party as individuals. Suppose, someone was to argue that the Iron and Steel Trades Confederation should cease having a political fund and its members should join the Labour Party as individuals. The writer of the article would wax fiercely indignant. He would point out that the Labour Party constitution permits the affiliation of trade unions and that the trade unions have a specific contribution to make to the Labour Party.

He would be right; but equally the Labour Party constitution permits the affiliation of Socialist societies; and a body of keen and enthusiastic Socialists like the Communist

Party, the largest of its kind in British history, has equally a contribution to make.

Indeed it is safe to say that one of the principal ways of bringing about decisive changes in public opinion is the activity of a party of individual members drawn from the more active trade unionists, shop stewards, co-operators and professional workers. Such a party is the Communist Party.

TRADE UNION RIGHTS

Both the trade unions and the Socialist societies have a distinctive role to play in the Labour Party. In opposing unity, the dominant leadership of the Laborer Party not only seeks to restrict the activity of affiliated political parties, but, as a necessary consequence of its policy, also restricts the political role of the trade unions.

Because of the great support given to it by its affiliated trade unions the Labour Party has sometimes been described as the "trade union in politics." Recent restrictions of trade union rights within the Party have, however, weakened the accuracy of this description. As a result of changes imposed in the period when the late Ramsay MacDonald was leading the Labour Party, the Labour Party, while prepared to accept the money of all trade unionists, is only prepared to give political rights to some trade unionists. Thus tens of thousands of Communists pay the political levy in the unions. The Labour Party takes that money but refuses to allow them to be delegates to local Labour Parties or the Labour Party Conferences or to be nominated as the Parliamentary candidates of the union. The offect of this policy is to create two classes of trade union members—those with full political and industrial rights and those with only industrial rights.

Thus Communists are Presidents, General Secretaries and National Organisers of trade unions but are not allowed to represent their union as delegates to the Labour Party, either on a national or a local basis. Ironically enough it is usually the

Communists who are in the forefront of campaigns to get all members of the trade unions to pay the political levy.

Consider, for example, these figures, which show the affiliation fees paid to the Labour Party by some important Trade Unions in 1935, and in 1942 (more recent figures are not available). In 1935 the Communist Party was not so strong and held fewer leading positions in these unions than in 1942. We are sure the 1943 figures will show an even bigger improvement:

	Dec. 1935	Dec. 1942
M.F.G.B.	£6,666	£8,588
A.S.L.E. & F.	£206	£362
N.U.R.	£3,468	£4,299
E.T.U.	£183	£333
A.E.U.	£1,166	£1,902
T. & G.W.U.	£4,128	£7,291
Nat. Union Foundry Workers	£132	£319
Fire Brigades Union	£10	£18

When the Communist Party was much less influential than it is to-day, it was possible for the Labour Party to get away with a policy which divided the unions into members with full rights and others. With the growth of Communist influence this policy is seen by all enlightened trade unionists as stupid, dangerous and destructive of trade union solidarity.

If the Labour Party were to agree to the affiliation of the Communist Party and to lift the ban against the Communists being allowed to represent their unions, working-class political unity would be achieved in a manner that is perfectly in keeping with the Labour Party constitution. Affiliation, not dissolution: this is the real way to working-class unity.

FACING BOTH WAYS

But Right-wing Labour men always want to have it both ways. They refuse to create a united Labour Movement by accepting Communist affiliation and yet expect the Communists to behave as if they were under Labour Party discipline.

"If there is no fundamental difference of policy," says the writer of the *Man and Metal* article, "there is no justification for the separate existence of the Communist Party. If, on the other hand, they claim that there is, they should seek power as a political Party, in their own way, on the basis of their own programme," he says.

Yet every honest Labour Pasty member knows that as soon as the Communists start seeking political power by putting up candidates, the writer in *Man and Metal* and those who share his views will promptly turn round and accuse the Communists of splitting the working-class vote. In any case there is no fundamental difference between the policy of the Communist Party for post-war Britain and that of the Labour Party; as readers of Harry Pollitt's book "How to Win the Peace" can find out for themselves.

WHICH GOVERNMENT?

Because the Communists are out for a Labour and Progressive Government at the next General Election they are anxious to avoid splitting the vote. They have tried to achieve unity of action through affiliation and it has been rejected. They are now trying to achieve it by means of an electoral agreement in which the various progressive parties agree to apportionment of seats and put their united weight behind a single candidate in each constituency.

Now, the writer in *Man and Metal* does not dare to deny that such unity might defeat the Tories:

> "If Electoral arrangements were made with the Communist Party and the result were a Labour Government, is there any guarantee from past history that the Communist Party would really support the Government they helped to return? On the contrary, the chances are that most of the time would be spent in holding the Government to ransom."

There you have a revelation of the outlook of an opponent of unity that should really worry a thinking trade unionist. For this writer is not concerned with a Tory Government being in power in Britain during the first formative years of peace. In effect he tells his readers that even if working-class unity can put a Labour Government in power it is not worth having because the Communists might work against such a Government.

But why should they? The Communists have been the most fervent advocates of unity in order to defeat Toryism. They will be interested more than anyone else in the progress of a Labour and progressive Government. So far from seeking to undermine it they will work to strengthen it in every possible way.

But what a damnable indictment of the anti-unity forces in the trade union movement. For what the writer in *Man and Metal* is really saying is "if we can only get a Labour Government with the aid of the Communists then we will do without a Labour Government." This is the attitude of people who are afraid of responsibility and power. They fear the post-war world and its problems and want to leave their solution to the Tories, hoping at most for a stronger Labour opposition to prevent the Tories from being too reactionary. The fact that unity would lead to a Labour and progressive victory is to such people an additional reason for opposing it.

But the great mass of trade unionists do not share the doubts and fears of those political weaklings. They want to see a great advance of the common people after the war and are determined on getting a Labour and progressive majority inside Parliament. That is why they should support unity between the Communist and Labour Parties, and consider exploring the possibility of electoral unity also with Common Wealth and Liberals.

UNIONS' CHOICE

The decision as to whether we will have progressive unity leading to a Labour and progressive majority in Parliament or whether we will have another Tory-dominated Parliament rests to a very great extent in the hands of the active trade unionists in this country. They have the power to break reactionary opposition to unity which threatens to saddle us with further long years of Tory domination.

Already great unions like the Amalgamated Engineering Union, the Mineworkers' Federation, the National Union of Railwaymen, the National Union of Distributive and Allied Workers have either declared in favour of Communist affiliation to the Labour Party or in favour of the Labour Party Executive meeting the Communist Party with a view to discussing joint action at the next General Election.

Most of the unions which were in favour of the Labour Party Executive meeting the Communist Party passed their resolutions after the agenda of the last Labour Party Conference was compiled. Consequently the discussion on unity which took place at the last Labour Party Conference was not raised in the most effective way.

There is still time between now and the next General Election to get the Labour Party to meet the Communist Party and other progressive bodies with a view to a united effort for a progressive victory at the General Election.

Between now and the General Election there will be another Labour Party Conference—at Whitsun, 1945. There is still time for trade unionists to win their unions for Unity, so that the Labour Party Conference gives instructions for electoral unity in order to defeat the Tories.

Between now and the General Election the annual or biennial conferences of many of the large unions will take place. If these Conferences spear for unity in no uncertain fashion the Labour Party Executive will be compelled to move.

So much that is vital to the trade union movement is at stake in the next General Election that progressive workers must work to achieve unity at all costs.

If a trade union were confronted with a strike, on the success of which its whole future depended, every conscientious trade unionist would work to ensure that the workers came out to the last man and woman.

The General Election will be vastly more important than any strike could possibly be. That is why trade unionists must support the unity policy which mobilises every man and woman to secure the decisive overthrow of Tory domination and the return of a Labour and progressive majority.

Remember, the trade union movement founded the Labour Party to conduct the political fight inside Parliament and in other ways on behalf of all working people.

In those days it was only a matter of winning a few Parliamentary seats; but to-day, with the trade union movement and Labour Party acting as leaders of the political and industrial life of the masses of the people of this coimtry, the question has become one of winning a decisive majority in Parliament, and of assuming the Governmental direction of this country.

The trade union movement, which fathered the Labour Party in 1900, must help its offspring to achieve power in 1945.

This means giving every help to build up the financial resources of the Labour Party in its fight against its rich opponent, the Tory Party. For every trade unionist, this involves the personal responsibility of paying the political levy; and campaigning to see that all trade unionists pay it, and supporting special grants towards the Labour Party funds from trade union resources.

It means rousing the trade union members to take a greater interest in the big political fight that will soon be upon us, to ensure that the trade union movement is solidly behind the policy of electoral unity against the Tories, and that every trade unionist uses his or her vote for Labour and Progressive candidates.

The trade union movement has it in its power to make certain that the end of this war will be quite different from the end of the last. It has it in its power to get the kind of Government that will give the people comfortable homes, give the children the best education, provide real health services and security for everyone, and transform this country into one of the world's leaders, equipped to provide the people with everything they need.

The age of scarcity has passed. Only the most narrow-minded self-seeking Tories wish to perpetuate the old days of cut-throat competition, unemployment and restricted production.

The Labour Party and Communist Party, with the active backing of the trade union movement, can make this the age of abundance, and lead the way in building that kind of Britain for which the men in the Services are fighting and

the workers in civil life are toiling.

Trade Union Leaders and the Labour Party

The Communist Party has proposed that the Labour Party should open discussions with other working-class and progressive organisations, with a view to ensuring the return of a Labour and progressive majority at the General Election.

In support of this proposal, one hundred and thirty-one individuals holding elected national positions in trade unions affiliated to the Labour Party, signed the following statement, which was sent to the Labour Party Executive:—

AS individuals holding elected national positions in trade unions affiliated to the Labour Party, we wish to put before your Executive Committee a point of view which we are confident is shared by large numbers of the members of our organisations.

The future of our working people, and indeed of the nation, depends on the Labour movement being roused to play its rightful part in leading the country, and putting through measures which will safeguard and promote the people's interests.

It cannot be seriously denied that, the Communist Party, with its active membership and campaigning energy, can greatly help the Labour Party in rallying the movement for its common aims.

The General Election is approaching, and the Communist Party has made a timely proposal to the Labour Party, to open discussions with, a view to ensuring the return of a Labour and progressive majority at the Election. We believe that, this proposal is in the interests of the whole movement, and we therefore urge you to give it favourable consideration, and not to allow past prejudices on either side to stand in the way of working-class unity and Labour's progress.

The signatories to this statement include nearly all the leading mining trade unionists in South Wales, Scotland, Lancashire and Cheshire; practically every member of the A.S.L.E. & F. Executive; seventeen out of the twenty-four members of the N.U.R. Executive; all but two of the E.T.U. Executive.

W. Lawther, W. J. Saddler, E. Hall, J. Hammond, A. L. Horner, Abe Moffatt, Alex Sloan, M.P., A. Davies, George H. D. Jenkins, Jim Evans, E. A. Bennet, J. Hughes, T. Lewis, S. B. Jones, J. Brookes, D. E. Thomas, J. W. Grant, E. J. Butler, J. W. Doder, James Evans, Cliff James, Joseph A. Hall, H. J. Finch, D. D. Evans, H. Lewis, R. H. Condon, W. Pearson, John Wood, Peter Henderson, John Colchart, Jas. Cook, Alex Cameron, John Rutherford, James Dickson, William Gray, Daniel Sim, James Tennyson, Alex Edgar, John Miller, A. N. Davidson, Malcolm Waugh, John Mitchell, Wm. Sneddon, Lawrence Glover, Harold Howarth.

Peter M'Cubbin, Fred Banner, D. F. Sharman, F. Kelland, G. W. Norton, H. E. Bidwell, A. W. Clifford, Ken Saunders, J. A. Brown, A. Barker, J. Harrison, L. H. Cronin, Thos. Hollywood, R. Hobbs, A. Ridyard, T. J. Rowan, A. R. Franks, J. H. Potts, Wm. Watson, H. R. Whitby, C. Rayner, C. Hoare, B. B. Lemoon, J. T. Owen.

W. Jeffcoate, Dan Wilson, W. B. Beard, Ted, Hill, C. A. Bean, Tom Rowlandson, A. Whitney, P. Doig, R. Airey, V. Stancy, S. H. Bradbury, George Ramage, C. Yates, W. Morgan, Jas. Duncan, G. Hutchings, G. Cole, L. Gregory, H. F. Ffoulkes, J. Hy. Potter, G. Stevens, H. J. Moorden, E. J. Haynes, T. Carter.

D. Groves, R. Bradds, S. Rise, R. G. Bowskill, E. Fletcher, J. Mooney, J. R. Scott, F. L. Haxell, E. Breed, Jack Deans, W. Stevens, M. S. Greenwell, E. Irwin, R. Henderson, D. G. Campbell.

J. Cullion, J.P., G. M. C. Robert, G. Mann, R. Barker, W. V. Donald, A. J. Gaynor, John Strain, Chas. Ratcliffe, A. Falconer, Phyllis Pimlott, J. R. Shanloy, Ken Baker, Frank Docherty, Arthur Fyles, J. H. Mills, S. Bishop, P. Belcher, Alfred Salkin, J. Gue, H. Kanter, Robert Milloy, James Parker, James Patterson.

A Socialist Solution to the Crisis

Concluding Speech at the Twentieth National Congress of the Communist Party

THIS Congress sees our Party stronger in numbers, firmer in discipline, more confident as to its way forward than any of the Congresses held since the termination of the war. We go forward from this Congress invigorated to smash the warmongers and to fight for the economic recovery and independence of our country. Without our Party the British people would be drifting into the greatest catastrophe in their history, a catastrophe causing endless pain and suffering.

Last year, many people saw the crisis in this country as being merely a temporary failure in our coal supply. They are now beginning to see it as a deep organic crisis of the whole capitalist system in Britain. We see a weakening of our imperialist basis and the loss of leadership in the capitalist world to the aggressive monopolists of the U.S.A. There is the effect of two terrible wars and the utter failure of the restrictive monopolies to modernise British industry between the wars. On top of this, there is the ruinous military expenditure, with which Britain has been saddled since 1945, which would be a crushing burden even in a prosperous country.

The consequences of all this will not be swept away in five minutes. It requires an organised effort under the leadership of a Left Labour Government, rejecting foreign domination, refusing to allow itself to be hampered by the Federation of British Industries, and mobilising our people to work for a free and independent Britain.

However deep the feeling against the Government, there is no inclination on the part of the British working class to turn to the Tories, with their policy of freeing the monopolists from the last vestige of control, their policy of creating mass

75

unemployment in order to impose the discipline of hunger on the common people of this land.

Dr. Dalton, in his broadcast, may have seen Churchill as the great war leader, though history will place a big question mark behind even that designation, but the people of this country remember him only too well as the ugly venomous reactionary who helped to break the General Strike and who would wade through seas of blood in a new world war against the Soviet Union and the New Democracies at the present day

Camouflaged Tory Policy

It is not enough to reject Churchill, Hudson and Eden. It is also necessary to guard against the dangers of a thinly-camouflaged Tory policy being gradually introduced into the Labour movement by Messrs. Attlee, Bevin, Morrison and Cripps.

We know that there are working people who appreciate some of the social reforms which the Government has placed on the statute book, who appreciate the shorter working week, who in the lower paid industries appreciate the increases in wages. But our Party has the duty to convince these workers that all these things which they are cherishing today are in jeopardy because of the failure of the Government to tackle the growing economic crisis. Indeed, all these things are being whittled away day by day by the Government itself.

Last week we saw the opening of an attempt to put a most brazen swindle across the working class of this country. The Government White Paper on wages was perfectly clear. No wage increases except in the undermanned industries. And when some undermanned industries apply they will be told, "Why, you've just had a wage increase—you've had it, chum." Freezing of wages. Refusal to peg prices. Refusal to increase the food subsidies. That is the Government's policy.

Of late, however, this line is being presented in a new

form. The T.U.C. tries to make us believe that the Government might be ready to bring down prices and to raise the wages of the lower paid. Dr. Dalton talks as if the whole object of the White Paper was to raise real wages, make the workers richer, and the rich poorer by enormous cuts in profits and by sharp reductions in prices. We regret to see that good progressive newspaper, *Reynolds News*, contributing to that prevailing confusion.

Will the trade union movement really believe that the capitalists who praise "Crippsian realism" can't read? Will the trade union movement really believe that what the Government is doing is to increase the purchasing power of wages and reduce the volume of profits?—and that the left wing are rejecting this veritable "manna from heaven"? We do not accept that interpretation of the White Paper, for the Government has made it perfectly clear there will be no increase in the food subsidies, and that the price freezing is on unessential goods.

Your food will rise in price, but the Government has given you the most definite promise to control the price of tooth-picks.

We are next told that the big Tory monopolists are being asked to reduce their own prices and profits. Blum tried it in France, and five minutes afterwards price ceilings rose so high that they could not be seen through a telescope even on a fine day. Truman tried it with private enterprise in the U.S.A., and after he had delivered his speech all his pals, including his doctor, gambled on the commodity markets, and pushed up prices still further.

Perhaps we are different in Britain. Perhaps for one bleak, Arctic smile from Sir Stafford Cripps the big boys of the F.B.I. will bring down the price ceilings, and restore happiness for evermore!

We tell the trade union movement that if it accepts the Government policy, it will be the policy as outlined in the White

Paper, not the gloss and misrepresentation being spread about the Government's intentions. The White Paper shows the Government is against any increases in food subsidies, against increasing low wages, and against cutting profits.

"Profligate Expenditure"

In his recent broadcast, Mr. Churchill talked about the country being ruined by "profligate expenditure." In his reply on the B.B.C., the good Dr. Dalton asked, was the rebuilding of Plymouth "profligate expenditure"? Was the new Health Service "profligate expenditure"? Was the financing of the Development Areas "profligate expenditure"? No, none of these things are "profligate expenditure," but it is precisely this expenditure which the Government is working to bring down to the lowest possible level. If Dr. Dalton wants an example of profligate expenditure, we can turn his attention to the military costs. In 1946 we had a trade deficit of £350 millions, and as against that no less than £382 millions were spent in that year on gross Government military expenditure overseas.

Even last year, the year of growing crisis, when we had a deficit of £675 millions in our balance of overseas payments, £209 millions of that was accounted for by this tremendous overseas military expenditure. Never in the whole of human history has a country suffering from such a dangerous deficit in its foreign balance carried such a weight of military expenditure.

"Britain's Plan for Prosperity"

Against all this we put our constructive policy contained in *Britain's Plan for Prosperity*—which is not a blue-print for the economic experts, but a programme of action for the whole working class.

The Labour Party does not know quite what to say about that plan. In the first days, the *Daily Herald*, through one, Mr.

78

McWhinnie, tried to belittle our plan by declaring that the modest production of consumer goods which we put forward alongside a great capital development programme, was a "flight of economic fancy." Now, last week, another "expert," a Mr. Donald Bruce, M.P., discovers that the large capital expenditure we are advocating can only be carried out by starving the British consumer for many years to come. What are the facts? We are suggesting a capital expenditure one-third above the pre-war rate—the same amount of capital expenditure as the Government's own experts were suggesting before the Government joined President Truman in the "cold war" against the Soviet Union, and gave up relying on the British people to work out their own salvation.

We will never put a flood of great new machines into the factories, we will never close the technical gap between our equipment and that of the U.S.A., never make our own key industries modern and efficient, unless we are prepared to mobilise our material and human resources to carry out such a great development programme as we have outlined in our plan. Mr. Bruce had better behave like his more illustrious ancestor who watched the persistent spider, and try again to produce a better argument against the Communist Plan for Prosperity.

In that plan we make suggestions for the allocation of our manpower. We have enough men and women in this country to build up our foreign trade, to increase our supplies of consumer goods, and to carry out the great capital development programme we have outlined here. We challenge our opponents to refute that, or to present an alternative manpower allocation that holds out hope for the British people.

There are two aspects of this plan underlined at this Congress. First, the need to nationalise steel by emergency decree, to raise the efficiency of this industry in the speediest possible way. It is a lie to say that the steel industry is an efficient industry. Only in one of the war years did its production ever reach the total it reached in 1937. Even if it reaches the Government's target this year, we will have little more than what was achieved eleven years ago. We will pay a full and bitter price in dependence upon America for the restrictive monopolist attitude of the steel barons. Instead of praising them for their efficiency we should denounce them and remove them. They have allowed this great asset of ours, the first great iron and steel industry in the world, to decline to the miserable state it is in at the present day.

Further, we want control of the engineering industry, so that the production of engineering machinery shall be concentrated to provide for the needs of the most vital industries. We have a great new machine in the mining industry, the power loader. In 1945 they were producing ten loaders per month. "Great strides" have been made since then, we are told, but the truth is that in December, 1947, we were producing only 13 loaders per month. As a contrast, the production of cigarette machinery is above pre-war! It is only in the last weeks that they have had the grace to send most of it abroad, and not to irritate the cigarette workers by installing new cigarette machinery to work up reduced stocks of tobacco.

Engineering is one of the great industries, in which there is no price control. And yet machinery is our greatest export. When a foreigner thinks of British prices, he does not think so much of the price of boots and shoes or Utility lipstick, he thinks in terms of generators, locomotives and tractors. These are enormously increasing in price, and we are being forced out of the market by the way some of the great engineering monopolies are raising the prices of these goods. We want a costing and efficiency system to bring these prices down to a reasonable level.

Communist Patriotism

Our Plan is based on confidence in the British people's ability to work their way out of the crisis. Our opponents say we are not a British Party. If we were, our M.P.s would show more respect for our ancient and traditional monarchy and our not so ancient monopolies. What rubbish! It is a queer kind of patriotism that bleats about the British Way of Life, but rejects the possibility of our great people, with their own skill, their own resources, discipline and working-class leadership, working out their own salvation in the modern world. Yet those Parties who utterly lack faith in the British people reproach the Communists for not being sufficiently patriotic! If the test of patriotism is wrapping the Union Jack around oneself to conceal the dollar sign, then we are not patriotic. If the test of patriotism is the desire to oppress others, then we are not patriotic. But if the test of patriotism is our willingness to work for the freedom, welfare and happiness of the common people of this land, then we claim to be the patriotic British Party above all others.

It is useless to say there are no strings attached to the Marshall Plan. There were no strings attached to the American Loan—but the ropes attached to it nearly strangled us! There are no strings attached to the Marshall Plan—there are chains and slavery attached to it instead. We are being treated as British imperialism in the eighteenth century treated the minor German States, who supplied the soldiers for British imperialist adventures in return for subsidies. For every penny we get under the Marshall Plan we will dissipate much more in maintaining a huge army, navy and air force to support American designs for the domination of Europe and the world.

John Mahon yesterday quoted England's great national poet, that never again would England lie at the proud foot of a conqueror. May I quote (with tiny variations) the national poet of the Scots, who characterised some of his own countrymen who sold their country for gold. "Such a parcel of rogues in a nation," he called them.

"What force or guile could not subdue
Through many warlike ages
Is wrought now by a coward few

81

For hireling traitor's wages.
The Nazi planes we could disdain,
Secure in valour's station,
But Yankee gold will be our bane,
Such a parcel of rogues in a nation."

It is bad enough to see trade unionists rushing to hug the Marshall chains themselves, pretending they are light, pretending they are not there—but it is surely monstrous to threaten the workers of other nations of the world that we will split the International Trade Union Movement because these workers will not wear the Marshall chains also. The American Federation of Labour is the chosen instrument of Wall Street. But let Deakin and Citrine be warned—the British workers are nobody's stooges. They were the first to recognise the young Soviet State as something new in the world; they protected it from imperialist intervention; they protected it by the threat of a General Strike during the Russo-Polish war of 1920. The British workers did a splendid job in raising the status of the colonial workers and in helping them to organise their trade unions, and in giving them advice as to how to develop their young Labour movement. Two of our comrades, George Allison and Ben Bradley, spent years in jail in India because of their efforts to help organise the trade unions there.

We will not allow these great links with the Russian and Colonial trade unions to be broken. Let Tewson and Deakin hear, not "His Marshall's Voice," but the voice of the British people, and let us keep International Trade Union Unity intact.

The discussion of the Communist Manifesto at this Congress has provided us with sharper weapons for the struggle that is ahead. Outside America, you know, capitalism is seldom defended as such today—it is Christian civilisation which is being defended by these "humble disciples" of the Master who had nowhere to lay his head. The big monopolists would have us believe it is not profit, it is not power, it is not their right to exploit they are defending, but their right to confess themselves as miserable sinners every Sunday morning. In order to rope a wider group into this so-called Christian civilisation, they sometimes call it Western civilisation, and even the Turks and the Japanese will in due time be classified as Westerners.

Class Consciousness is the Key

We ask our Labour friends not to think in terms of religion, but to think in terms of class. If they did that, they would never be deceived by this East-West nonsense. If Messrs. Attlee and Morrison have forgotten, most workers know that there are progressive classes in our society, moving forward, and there are reactionary classes striving to preserve the decaying social order.

We see the working class today in the Soviet Union treading the road from Socialism to Communism, and we see the New Democracies building up Socialism, each in their own particular way. The great mass Communist Parties of France and Italy represent the majority of workers in these countries. When Messrs. Attlee and Morrison call for a crusade against Communism, they call for a crusade against the majority of the European working class, they call for a crusade against the progressive forces in the world.

Where are the millionaires in this struggle? Where are the quislings? Where is fascist big business? Where are the feudal landlords? Organised around Wall Street: organised around the campaign of reaction, boosting the policy of Western Union.

Are we going to allow the British working class, the children of the Chartists, of the Co-operators, of the Tolpuddle Martyrs, and the great pioneer organisers of the Socialist movement, to be brought into the campaign of blackest reaction against their own natural allies? No, comrades, we will need to convince our Labour Party friends that their duty is in the camp of their own class, the camp of the Soviet Union, the camp of

Czechoslovakia, where our Party will triumph in this crisis, the camp of the working class advancing all over Europe and of the advancing colonial peoples.

And before Mr. Attlee gives us any more sermons about free expression in Britain, let him read the evidence before the Press Commission of how Francis Williams, the pre-war editor of the *Daily Herald*, had constantly to obey orders from millionaire Lord Southwood, who controlled the commercial side of that particular undertaking. But we are no longer dependent on the *Daily Herald*. This year you will see, after many disappointments, but this time certainly, a great new *Daily Worker*.

We should appreciate this great new weapon which we have forged with our own sacrifices. Do not treat it lightly. What would the pioneers of Socialism have given for such a weapon?

What would our life be today without it as we face the daily struggle in the interests of our class?

A Stronger Communist Party

In the teeth of the witch hunt our Party is strengthening its influence in the unions and increasing its members. We have had some reports regarding the magnificent progress made in bringing more members into our Party. If time had allowed, we would have had more, all telling the same story. That story is that there are no longer any difficult areas in this country for the Communist Party. We have gone beyond the days when we were confined to London and the Celtic fringe of South Wales and Scotland.

The days are gone when we were mainly a Party of the unemployed, when we had no weight in the great industries, in the great unions, when we had no weight with the progressive intelligentsia. But great as our achievements have been, we must make them greater in 1948. We have got to change the mood of doubt and grumbling in the Labour movement into active opposition to the present policy, against Marshall slavery, against the Western Union.

There can be no Western European bridgehead against the progress of Socialism in Europe without the British people. We are, therefore, a decisive sector. If we smash the warmongers here, the whole campaign of Wall Street and reaction elsewhere will be thrown out of gear. France and Italy will be relieved of the pressure now upon them if we do our duty in this country.

When the Prime Minister gives three speeches in succession denouncing the Communist Party, when he is reinforced by the viperish stupidity of the ex-Prime Minister, that is a compliment to our Party, to our work, to our influence in this country. It is an indication to us that we are a greater force than we imagined that we ought not to underestimate ourselves, that not tens of thousands, but millions, are beginning to lend a receptive ear to our message.

From this Congress we go forward to make our Party one of the principal Communist Parties in Europe, and the world, a Communist Party winning a decisive victory in the most decisive sector at the present time. A Communist Party making a mighty contribution to the peace and freedom of all mankind.

Reply to Discussion

I WANT TO deal with the following points which have been raised in discussion: How we handle the question of the fight against the crisis; how we develop the mass movement; the issue of the General Election; the battle of ideas, and the role of the Party.

Now, of course, none of us are under any doubt that the crisis will develop, that the cost of living will go up six, seven, or even ten points, that unemployment will grow in the basic industries of this country. But I think we have got to avoid the tendency of analysing the crisis as spectators, and start really acting on the crisis as militant workers.

We tend to be more expert in analysing the crisis than moving and rousing the fight against it. We are not astrologers and fortune tellers, foretelling to the workers their sad future; we are agitators and organisers, full of confidence and optimism, convincing the workers that if they fight, their future will never be a sad one.

Our only safeguard against the crisis lies in developing the workers' fight. We know from some of our reports that there are Party members in factory groups who are meeting the crisis by lying low. They are "protecting the factory group", they say. This is the surest means of securing victimisation of every member of the factory group. Maintaining factory organisation in the fight is the only way to safeguard the individual.

Therefore I commend the action of the shipbuilding workers and the women of Nelson, of whom we have heard from this platform. They have demonstrated that they are not waiting for the full impact of the crisis—they are getting their blows in first; they are reacting against the first, tiny manifestations of increasing, unemployment, and we want that to be a lesson to other workers.

In this situation we have got to draw a clear line between the reformist leaders and the Labour Party workers. It is one of the most important aspects of Comrade Pollitt's report, to which too little attention has been paid in the discussion. The Labour workers want what we want; they want full employment, and the removal of the menace of victimisation from the militants; they want no cuts in real wages, but an advance in wages towards a higher standard of living. They want no cuts in social services, but their expansion. They want powerful unions under democratic control of the membership. The leaders want all that the Labour workers do not want-prices rising without wages increasing, no increase in wages until prices are up by six points further.

Every worker has had his wages docked by 6s. or 7s. per week; every union going forward for wage increases is hampered by the trade union instruction to employers and to Arbitration Tribunals that wage increases ought not to be granted until real wages have been reduced a bit further, until the cost of living is up a few more points.

The reformist leaders want to keep housing down to the miserable level of 175,000 next year, half the level of a good pre-war year in housing construction. And we must arouse the workers against this. We must get the women indignant; we must tell the demagogue Bevan that his prefabricated insults to the Tories are not a substitute for houses for the British people to live in.

In the eighteen months up to devaluation, the reformist leaders represented themselves as having an alternative policy to the Communists. Whenever we came forward for increased. wages, they brought forward alternative proposals to reduce food prices as the alternative to increased wages. When we rejected the Cripps policy in 1948, they promised an early fall in the cost of living—and Cripps increased the tax on tobacco and withdrew the leather and wool subsidies and pushed prices up. When we rejected the policy of the T.U.C. in 1948, Cripps followed by the increase in prices through the pegging of the food subsidy in the budget this year. When they reaffirmed this policy in September 1949, it was immediately followed up by devaluation, meaning a substantial cut in the standard of life of all the people in this country.

We are not fighting merely for wage standards. We are fighting for the very existence of the Trade Union movement as a democratic institution controlled by its members. We object to the policy of taking the control out of the hand of the members of the unions and putting it under distant control from Wall Street. Wall Street imposed devaluation and the Government immediately proceeds to ask the unions to wipe out the democratic decisions of their members; to break up the trade union cost of living agreements; to cease to defend their members.

The British unions are now being tied up more than any unions have ever been in so-called capitalist democracy. The General Council tells the Arbitration Tribunals to refuse wage increases. If a union rejects this advice, there is still the machinery of compulsory arbitration to force it to conform. Hitler imposed wage cuts by destroying trade unions; British Social Democracy seeks to impose them by distortion of the Trade Union movement and by the destruction of trade union democracy.

We have faith that the British working class will destroy this traitor policy utterly. The British working class may be cautious and slow moving, but when it gets its hands on something like a standard of life, like a guaranteed week, like a social reform, it is easier to take a chunk of meat out of the jaws of a bulldog than to take these things away.

This may be a slow-moving working class. It may be far too practical-minded for its own benefit; but it is the working class which forced the trembling reformist leaders into the General Strike of 1926, it is the working class that built up the miners with their seven months' strike; and comrades will know that this year it was the British dockers from Avonmouth, Bristol, and London whose long, hard fight on behalf of the Canadian seamen set an example of international working-class solidarity.

No one can fight like the British workers when they are roused, and no one can fight like the British women when they are roused. It was the British women who fought the fight for votes for women in the days just previous to the First World War. It is the British women who are the backbone of the rent agitation in various parts of the country today.

Some comrades say: "Yes, we would do better in our trade union fight if we weren't running so many candidates at the General Election. The Labour workers don't like it. Perhaps if we were more 'tactical' we would get better results in the economic field." But, even if the General Election has not been discussed, I ask our comrades to reflect on the fact that if we were not running 100 candidates, who would be carrying on the fight for Britain's independence in the General Election?

It seems almost like yesterday when Labour leaders were telling us we were carrying no hampering obligations under the Marshall Plan. Since then, in return for Marshall dollars, we have had to subordinate ourselves as war allies of the United States, pouring out resources for war and cutting housing, to provide these resources. Lancashire has been turned into a war base for the American atom; planes; since then we have had to tolerate the U.S. Treasury organising the financial crooks of the whole world, from Wall Street to Tangiers and Cairo, in an attack on the British £.

Now they are going to try and drive us into the same kind of arrangement by the U.S. low-wage satellites in Europe. European tariffs have to be lowered to make that continent—or the western part of it—a vast market for U.S. goods. The U.S. gangster manipulation of customs regulations has got to remain, and very shortly, if we don't stop it—and we will stop it—we will find amongst our allies the West German army, dominated

90

by those same Nazi types whom we fought in 1945 and thought we had crushed for ever. No Nazi gauleiters behaved as crudely as Hoffman and Harriman are behaving in relation to this country at the present moment.

We would be traitors to the British people if we did not fight against this policy. What kind of a Communist Party would we be if we did not fight against the subjection of Britain to the monopolists of the U.S.A.? How could we hold up our heads in the great world-wide family of the Communist Parties if we did not make the General Election the occasion for a fight for the defence of the Soviet Union and the establishment of peace throughout the world? If we were not to make that fight, the electoral contest would be a fight between two parties discussing who was best equipped to fight Communism; who was best equipped to lead towards the Third World War.

Mr. Hector McNeil dared to tell Vyshinsky that world opinion was more united against the Soviet Union than it has been against Herr Hitler. This is a lie in the best Goebbels tradition.

It tells us nothing about world opinion, of the opinions of the masses in the colonies, of the great emancipated workers and peasants of Eastern Europe, of the great Communist Parties in the West. It tells us nothing about world opinion; but it illuminates the psychopathology of Social Democracy in this country and its frantic hatred of people building up Socialism while it is retreating before the American millionaires.

George Short told us that one of their characteristics was to make a Left speech as a prelude to surrender. Nye Bevan tells the workers in Middlesbrough that the steel masters can no more run the steel industry than his granny. Nine days afterwards the steel masters are reprieved even from the phoney nationalisation of this Government. But reprieved men and reprieved institutions sometimes live long. Unless we are arousing the workers at the General Election, the steel monopoly in this country might survive as long as Nye Bevan's granny to exploit and rob the people of this country.

Then there is Manny Shinwell, who puts out his tongue at the financial oligarchy of the City of London (from a safe distance), and that is followed by the nationalisation of insurance being transformed into the mutualisation of insurance, or the mutilisation of insurance, as one indignant Labour Party member put it.

These retreats are forced on the British Government by its allies and partners, by the British monopolists with whom it hopes to co-operate and its ally, U.S. imperialism.

There is a group of M.P.s going shortly to Yugoslavia. They are going to discover whether Tito, on, the basis of American loans and the American stranglehold, is building up Communism in Yugoslavia or not. I don't know why they are going to Belgrade for information on this point. All the necessary data is there for them to see in Westminster and in Whitehall.

This shows that under the grip of the American monopolists, not only can one not build up Socialism, but one cannot carry through the mildest of democratic deforms, and one is forced to pursue a policy that means the complete ruination of one's own country. And the best argument against Tito is that the architect of the Fulton policy, Mr. Winston Churchill, is convinced that he is no longer a Communist.

The General Election will help us a thousandfold in our economic struggle—because every one who has been in an economic struggle knows that the workers are being held back, as Will Paynter said, by political inhibitions, by misunderstandings of Soviet policy, by misrepresentations of what the Communists stand for in this country; and the more we use the General Election to clear the air the greater the struggle on the economic field will be.

The economic struggle and the political struggle are part of the one process. They are not in contradiction to one another, and we ask all members, from the most important trade union officials to the most recently joined recruit, to make the General Election the greatest fight in which our Party has ever engaged.

Douglas Garman's point was that the Battle of Ideas is not a battle between professors. We must attack all the main trends of bourgeois ideology, logical positivism, Mendel-Morgan genetics, Keynesian economics, which have polluted the Labour movement from top to bottom, but we must also fight those more crude ideas which have such an influence over the masses at the present time.

Julie Jacobs was right when he said we cannot advance the cause of British workers unless we kill every anti-Soviet lie, in the language of Bunyan, of Cobbett, of Blatchford, and Gallacher and Pollitt, and not in a jargon far above the head of the masses of the people in this country.

Lastly, we must strengthen our Party, not only by criticism and self-criticism, but by turning outside to the workers. Let us measure our Party influence by the number of actions we have led, by the number of non-Party workers we have approached in a given week, by the mounting sales of the *Daily Worker*. Heroic words require to be matched by heroic deeds. Force up the circulation of our paper, which is the sharpest weapon in the hands of the Party.

Self-criticism must strengthen and not weaken the discipline of the Party. According to certain sections of the press Harry Pollitt says we are not sufficiently following up the line of the Extended E.C. in February. All the other material of the struggle of the British workers by our constructive policy is passed over to Harry Pollitt's criticism. Therefore things must be in a bad way. Truly things would be in a terrible way if we ever got the philosophy, if we ever thought we were doing everything that was possible.

The Right-Wing sneer at our discipline—but while they, sneer they envy.

We know that social changes are not made by exhibitionists, but by great mass movements, and not stimulated by poseurs and political one-man bands, but by organised workers under the leadership of a disciplined Party such as ours. And it is not such a mechanical discipline, but a free discipline of free men and women in which their service is to their class. And therefore we will go into great battles, and we will emerge strengthened, with greater numbers and a wider circulation for our paper, and greater influence over the mass of our people; and the mass of the people will emerge from the economic struggles, from the General Election, from the fights of the women, strengthened and influenced by our example.

Neither press conspiracies of silence will deter us in our fight. Our greatest hour as a Communist Party is approaching. We shall go forward joyfully to match that confidently, knowing that we take the British working class a long way along the road, making this land a great bastion in the triumphant family of Socialist nations.

Socialism for Trade Unionists

The trade unions are the foundation of the Labour Party. They supply the greater part of its finance. Their members are the most stable and reliable section of the Labour voters. They must not be ignored in the formulation of Labour Party policy. So the Right Wing trade union leaders have been emphasising, ever more stridently, since the Labour Party conference in Morecambe last year.

At the Morecambe conference of the Labour Party, through their spokesmen Messrs. Deakin and Lawther, the Right Wing leaders threatened those elements of the Labour Party who were striving for a policy which would be an advance on that which the Right Wing leaders were operating. When a number of supporters of Mr. Aneurin Bevan were elected to the Party Executive, the anger of those leaders expressed itself in the most unmitigated bullying of the local Labour parties.

The latest and most alarming expression of this hostility is the refusal of the General Council of the Trades Union Congress to co-operate closely with the Labour Party in the formulation of a statement of policy. This despite a Right Wing majority on the latter body.

The main "crime" of the Constituency Labour Parties at Morecambe was that they were demanding that Britain should cease to allow itself to be towed in the wake of the United States of America in matters of foreign policy; that the nationalised industries should be reorganised, and that the workers should have a real say in their administration. So far from the process of nationalisation being halted, as the Right Wing leaders asserted that it should, they were insisting on the further nationalisation of Britain's great monopolies.

These are the views which the Right Wing trade union leaders will seek to manipulate their conferences into rejecting this year. We believe that if the conferences do so they will be striking a very deadly blow against the interests of their own members, and we propose to say why.

Why Trade Unions?

The Trade Union Movement is based on the proposition that the workers by hand and brain, who sell their services to the capitalist class—*i.e.*, the owners of industry—have interests which are opposed to those of that class. Trade unions were formed because the workers, by bitter experience, found that the capitalists were driven, by the necessities of their system, to extract the greatest amount of work for the lowest amount of wages from those they employed. Unions were therefore formed to establish standard rates of wages, to limit the working hours, and otherwise to improve the standards of the workers.

Unions and the Law

Trade unionists were not long in discovering that the State was not a neutral body representing the interests of the community. It constantly intervened against the workers in strikes. It passed legislation which hindered the growth of trade unionism. Its judges gave the law a twist, interpreting it to the detriment of the workers, as in the famous Taff Vale decision in 1901.

So just as the capitalist system compelled the workers to form unions in self-protection, so the behaviour of the capitalist State forced the unions to interest themselves in politics and form the Labour Party. Trade unionists were encouraged and helped to form the Labour Party by the propaganda and activities of various Socialist bodies like the Social Democratic Federation, the Socialist League of William Morris, and the Independent Labour Party.

For as the capitalist system developed, the most alert sections of the workers began to see that not only had the capitalist class different interests than they had, but that the capitalist system, and not merely particular groups of capitalists, was the workers' deadly enemy. Every ten years or so the capitalist system collapsed in a great economic crisis. Millions of workers became unemployed, and the capitalist class used that situation to depress wages and to break up trade union organisation. This happened most strikingly in the great economic crisis which followed the first world war. In 1920, for example, the number of trade unionists affiliated to the Trades Union Congress stood at 6,500,000. By 1929 it was down to 3,673,000. Trade union militants were victimised in workshop after workshop and trade union organisation was broken up. Many of the gains made by the workers in periods of good employment were lost. It therefore became increasingly clear to the advanced workers that if the working class had to defend their standard of life it was necessary to win political power and abolish capitalism.

What Socialism Means

The transformation of Capitalism to Socialism meant amongst other things:—

That political power should pass from the hands of the capitalist class into the hands of the working people. The more far-sighted workers realised that this meant not merely a Parliamentary majority, but that all the key positions in the State administration should be in the hands of trusted members of the working people.

That the means of production and distribution, the land, the factories, workshops and mines, the means of communication, the financial system, should pass into the possession of the working people.

That production should be developed not by the

97

competition of the various capitalist enterprises for profit, but on the basis of a planned economic system, whose aim was to raise the material and cultural level of the people.

That the national income should be distributed in such a way as to raise the standards of the working people and to enlarge the productive power of the Socialist industries, and not, as it is under capitalism, to enrich a powerful class of capitalists and their hangers-on.

That the continued improvement of the standard of life of the working people would be a stimulus to ever-increasing production and would be a guarantee against crises of overproduction, with all the mass unemployment which these entailed.

In other words, the working people would own the industries, plan the industries and work for themselves and not for the capitalist class.

This was the Socialist outlook which the advanced workers in the Labour Party propagated amongst their fellows right from the formation of the party.

So in the wake of the first world war and the Russian revolution there was embodied in the constitution of the Labour Party in 1918 the following aim:—

"To secure for the workers by hand, or by brain, the full fruits of their industry and the most equitable distribution thereof that may be possible, upon the basis of the common ownership of the means of production, distribution and exchange and the best obtainable system of popular administration and control of each industry and service."

The general outlook behind this policy has been defined by Mr. Gaitskell, one of the Right Wing leaders, as follows:—

"Injustice was regarded as due to the payment of profits, dividends and interest-unearned income. Therefore, the argument ran, take over the means of production, stop this flow of unearned income altogether (save perhaps for some compassionate allowances)." (*Political Quarterly*, Jan./March, 1953).

Mr. Gaitskell does not agree with this policy which he is here outlining, but it is useful to have his reminder that in the minds of Labour's pioneers the original objects of nationalisation were to stop capitalist exploitation—*i.e.*, "the payment of profits, dividends and interest"—and to provide a basis for economic planning.

There is nothing in common between such Socialist nationalisation and that exemplified in pre-war days by the Post Office, the British Broadcasting Corporation and the Central Electricity Board. The object of capitalist nationalisation is not to lay the foundations of a new society. It is to provide an efficient State auxiliary service for the industries which remain in private hands.

The nationalisation of coal and power, transport and steel undertaken by the Labour Government was of this type. As Mr. Gaitskell admits, it

". . . does not stop the flow of unearned income: all that happens is that it takes the form of a smaller and more certain form of interest payments instead of a larger but much less certain profit income." (*Political Quarterly*, Jan./March, 1953.)

When one takes the greater certainty of interest income over a period it is doubtful if the return is in any way smaller. The object of this type of capitalist nationalisation is to provide cheap transport and power and other services for the capitalist class. The tests of genuine Socialist nationalisation are:—

1. That trusted representatives of the workers are in the key positions of the State administration; and

2. The major role which the unions perform in individual industries and in relation to the plan. The trade unions participate in the administration of the nationalised industries, nationally, regionally, and in every factory. They participate in drawing up the economic plan which allows for steadily advancing wages and conditions.

It is this conception of genuine nationalisation, based on the conquest of political power by the working class, which should guide trade unionists in all their work.

Since the Labour Party constitution was accepted in 1918 a Socialist society has come into existence in the Soviet Union. Applying the principles of Marxism and Leninism, the Soviet Union has transformed itself from a country with a backward, and in part mediæval technique, into a great dynamic Socialist State based on the most advanced technique. It was no Communist, but ex-President Truman who said recently: "The United States and the Soviet Union had emerged after the last war as the two strongest powers in the world." (Message on the State of the Union, January 8, 1953.)

There were not in the Soviet Union before 1923 any substantial iron and steel industry, any automobile or tractor industry, any agricultural machinery industry, any aircraft or chemical industry. Now all these industries exist on a large and growing scale. The industrial output of the Soviet Union has increased 12 times since 1929, while in the same period that of the U.S.A. has doubled, that of Britain is two-thirds higher, that of France is 4 per cent. higher and that of Italy one-third higher. In this period capitalism has suffered a tremendous unemployed depression and has brought upon the world a vast and destructive war.

The majority of Right Wing leaders, however, have at the best only paid lip-service to the Socialist aim of the Labour Party. It was never a guide to their daily practice.

Nevertheless it remained the official objective of the Party. It is this objective which the rank and file insist should determine the day-to-day actions of the Party and which the Right Wing trade union leaders want to reduce to an empty formula, having no influence on policy at all.

Capitalism and War

Socialists have always criticised the capitalist system because it gave rise not only to recurring economic crises, but to ever more devastating wars.

When the Labour Party was formed in 1900 the Boer War was raging. This war was opposed by the new Labour Party on the ground that it was a war on behalf of the capitalist owners of the gold and diamond mines, who believed that their investment would be safer under a British imperialist government than under the governments of the Boer Republics. This war was followed by the Russo-Japanese war for markets and territory in the Far East, by clashes, between Germany and Britain in the Middle East (the Berlin-Baghdad railway), by conflicts between Germany and France over Morocco, by the struggle between Russia and Austria-Hungary in Central Europe. The naval race between Germany and Britain dominated British foreign policies in the decade before 1914. Out of these clashing capitalist interests came the war of 1914-18. The imperialist character of this war was underlined by the character of the peace settlement—Germany and Turkey were stripped of their colonies, which became "mandated territories" or "spheres of influence" of the victorious powers. The Second World War arising out of the imperialist ambitions of Germany and Japan and Italy likewise emphasised that wars had their roots in the capitalist system of society. The connection between the economic crises of 1929-33 and the expansionist policy of Nazi Germany was recognised by everyone.

Now the Socialist theory that capitalism (especially in its monopoly stage) gives rise to wars, which is based on generations of experience, is being disputed by the Right Wing of the Labour Party. The greatest of all capitalist nations, the United States of America, is declared by those leaders to be inherently peaceful. If it strives to cut the ties binding capitalist Britain to its colonies and dominions, this is held to be a proof of its desire for peace. If it seeks to rearm the German and Japanese militarists and bring them into its war alliance, it is only showing its peaceful intentions. If it subsidises General Franco and makes him its ally, it does so only in the interests of democracy. Kit seizes Chinese territory (Formosa) and prepares for an attack on the People's Republic of China, it is merely resisting aggression. If it encircles the Soviet Union and China with atom bomb bases it is only defending itself. If it compels European countries to adopt arms programmes of such a magnitude that they disorganise the economic life of the countries concerned, it is only giving friendly advice.

The Challenge to Socialism

So the Right Wing leaders are challenging Socialist principles on two main points. They are denying that it is necessary for society to take over all the main industries in order to plan for the welfare of the people (they say that all that is necessary is the existing nationalisation plus some State control) and they are denying that monopoly capitalism (imperialism) in its struggle for markets and sources of raw materials, in its struggle to oppress the workers and the colonial peoples in order to obtain maximum profits, is really the cause of war.

The Right Wing Labour leaders point to the fact that there is at present no general mass unemployment, that a great system of social security has been established, that the school-leaving age has been raised and the hours of labour have been reduced. It is possible, they argue, for further improvements to be made as production increases from year to year.

Now there can be no doubt that the working class have wrung the above-listed reforms from the capitalist class. In the course of the war against Fascism and in the immediate post-war period the workers were able to force the ruling class to grant concessions.

Does this constitute a definite and fundamental social change, built on sound foundations, a social change that is a basis for further advance? The Right Wing leaders say that it does. Those who adhere to Socialist principles say that it does not. They say that the capitalist system is moving into new crises and that in those crises the post-war gains of the working class will be in great danger.

Post-War Gains in Danger

Slowly but nevertheless surely the purchasing power of wages has been falling. Since June, 1947, male wage rates have risen by 32 per cent. In the same period the retail price index has risen by 38 per cent. (December, 1952). If the trade unions had not ignored the wage freeze and maintained a powerful pressure for increased wages, the disparity would have been still greater.

Still greater is the fall in the purchasing power of social service payments—sickness benefit, unemployment benefit and industrial injuries benefit. Those payments were first fixed in July, 1946, and were increased by 25 per cent. By the Chancellor of the Exchequer in 1952. The cost of living in the same period has increased by 43 per cent. So that the very basis

103

of the much vaunted social services is being washed away. State control is not protecting the gains of the workers even when employment remains good.

Up till recently it was being said that there was no need to take the major industries out of the hands of the capitalist class in order to lay the basis for economic planning for welfare and for full employment; that a Labour government, by establishing control over privately owned industry, could compel that industry to conform to a national plan. For example, Mr. Herbert Morrison at the Morecambe Labour Party conference said "whether publicly or privately owned the management (of industry) must be made to play the game by the public interest and so must the workers: all industry must." (1952 *Labour Party Conference Report*, p. 110.) Obviously, if managements of privately owned industries can be made by State control to play the game by public interest, the need for abolishing the private ownership of industry is reduced.

Now no one denies that State control (which in practice means control in the interests of the dominant group of the capitalists) can work for a limited period. It is effective enough, in the short run, in preventing some capitalists from doing what they want to do. It can, for example, stop capitalists from building cinemas by refusing them building licences. State control cannot, however, force capitalists to do what they don't want to do because they see no profit in it. It cannot force textile firms to expand their activities instead of contracting them. At the present moment, for example, Platt Bros., the famous textile machinery firm, is dismissing workers. Yet many sections of the British textile industry are working with obsolete, worn-out machinery.

Mr. Harold Wilson, ex-President of the Board of Trade, has testified to private capitalism's continued and successful efforts to evade the Government's investment plans. (*In Place of Dollars*, p. 15.) The capitalists are always discovering new ways to evade controls.

The Fight for Work

A clear illustration of the incompatibility of private ownership of the major industries with economic planning is seen in relation to the aim of full employment.

Higher money wages and lower prices are the way in which a Socialist society increases the purchasing power in the hands of the people. Private enterprise will, however, only maintain employment provided it sees the continuing possibility of maximum profits. It can only secure those profits by limiting or preventing wage increases, *i.e.*, by preventing the purchasing power of the people from expanding and thereby providing an ever-growing outlet for all the goods which can be produced. The drive of private monopolies for profits is thus in direct contradiction with the need to increase the purchasing power of the people as the basis of a genuine policy of full employment. So it happens that the increase of production is always coming up against the limited consuming power of the people, with the result that the goods produced cannot be cleared off and mass unemployment results. The slump in the textile industry was not merely due to the loss of foreign markets for textiles. It was also due to the collapse of the home market.

In order to defend living standards the workers must do everything in their power to force up wages (and to overcome the resistance of Right Wing leaders to this policy); they must compel the capitalist State to engage in all kinds of work schemes; but, in the last analysis, if they want to avoid devastating economic crises they must take the major industries out of the hands of the capitalists, so that those industries can become the basis of a genuine economic plan—a plan which ensures that consumption (wages and social services) keep pace with production, so that there is no crisis of over-production leading to mass unemployment.

The Achievements of Socialism

In contrast to the growing fears of unemployment,

British trade unionists should note the splendid post-war achievements of the Socialist system in the Soviet Union.

There was no country so heavily devastated in the war: 31,850 factories, mills and other industrial enterprises (exclusive of small plants) were wrecked. Yet by 1948 the pre-war industrial level was restored as the basis for a rapid advance. By 1952 Soviet industry was producing 15 million tons of steel per year additional to that which it produced in 1940—an addition to Soviet steel production which almost equalled the entire product of the British steel industry in 1951. Coal production in 1952 was 134 million tons additional to that of 1940—an addition which represents three-fifths of the entire annual British coal output.

These results have not been obtained by keeping down living standards. The real income of the workers in 1952 was 57 per cent. higher than in 1940. To-day the Soviet Union, advancing towards Communism, has, amongst other things, set itself the task of doubling real wages and reducing the hours of labour to six per day. The shadow of an economic crisis does not darken that land. No better example could be afforded as to the ability of Socialism to evoke the constructive enthusiasm of the people to achieve inspiring results.

Paying Our Way

All this fine talk of advancing to Socialism is all very well, the Right Wingers say, and no doubt if Britain were like the Soviet Union, a comparatively self-supporting country, such a programme could be carried out. But Britain is heavily dependent on the world market. It is barely able to pay for the food that is needed by its people and for the materials which are required by its industries. Therefore this balance-of-payments crisis has first to be solved. All these fine schemes for nationalising Britain's monopolies have very little to contribute to solving this problem. This was the essence of Mr. Herbert Morrison's argument at the Morecambe conference. Of course nationalisation by itself—even if it is genuine Socialist nationalisation-must be part of a wider policy. Nevertheless it is an integral part.

We must remember that Britain last year spent £350 million on overseas military expenditure arising from the wars in Korea and Malaya, and the garrisoning of the Middle East. That £350 million is paid for by British exports, which are therefore used not merely, to provide the means of purchasing foreign food and raw material but to carry on wars. If Britain granted the colonial peoples their independence and ceased to make war on them, it would improve its ability to pay its way. That is why the Right Wing defence of imperialism means the betrayal of this country.

Further, Britain is allowing its imperialist boss, the United States of America, to restrict its right to send certain types of engineering goods to the Soviet Union, China and Eastern Europe. It is using a large part of its engineering industry to produce arms instead of exports. It is thus diminishing its ability to pay its way in the world. This is the consequence of its participation in an imperialist war alliance directed against the Socialist Soviet Union. If Britain abandonded this alliance it would be in a better position to balance its accounts with the outside world.

It is not enough to abandon those imperialist policies which are destroying Britain's trade. There must be in addition a deliberate planning of foreign trade, which in turn requires the national ownership and the national economic planning of Britain's industries. It is not sufficient to free Britain's engineering industries from the burden of rearmament. It is necessary to gear them to a vast production plan to meet the needs of our actual and potential customers, and also to supply the vast amount of equipment which is necessary for making British industry in general more efficient.

It is, for example, essential that British industry should supply the Dominions with equipment which they now obtain from the U.S.A. It is no good imploring Australia, New Zealand, South Africa, India and Pakistan to forgo capital goods of American origin if they cannot guarantee British capital goods of the quality and quantity required. If Britain expects the Soviet Union and Poland to deliver supplies of coarse grain, wheat and timber on time, it must in turn ensure that British capital goods are also delivered on time. A great deal of trade must be done by means of long-term contracts between governments.

Thus the engineering industry must be brought under a form of Socialist nationalisation and concentrated on the major purposes of re-equipping British industry and making a decisive contribution to the export trade. We also need the nationalisation of shipbuilding and chemicals, the banks and the insurance companies, and the land of the big landowners.

Only when such a substantial portion of industry is in the hands of the State can there be an advance to a real planned attack on Britain's major problems.

The capitalist government seeking to drive private industry to export more does so by tightening credit and restricting purchasing power on the home market. The reduced home market, based on unemployment, will, it is hoped, drive the capitalists in sheer self-preservation to capture a larger share of the foreign markets. Thus the alternative to planned foreign trade is an export drive founded on the weapon of unemployment in the industries catering for domestic demand.

This would be a plausible policy if one capitalist country alone were engaged in it. When, however, all capitalist countries simultaneously engage in it, the result is to increase unemployment all round.

Unions and Socialism

The Right Wing leaders want to use the unions to support them in continuing the present imperialist policy, in refusing to reorganise the nationalised industries, in halting further nationalisation, and in insisting that the State can induce private monopolies to work for the public good. In short, they want the Labour Party to adhere to a position indistinguishable, in practice, from that of the Tory Party.

If trade unionists are not prepared to connive at the destruction of their organisations they have utterly to defeat this policy.

This means that every trade union branch has got to be affiliated to the Labour Party and to send delegates who will fight for the adoption of a progressive policy for advance to Socialism. It means that this fight must be actively waged in every trade union conference this year. The adoption of a progressive policy is vital to trade union survival.

At the same time the unions must seek to increase their membership, draw more workers into daily participation in their work and create a genuine democracy inside every union. For more than a parliamentary majority is necessary, if the capitalist class in the major industries is to be dispossessed. The unions will require to be at their posts, powerful, united and militant, ready to break the resistance of the capitalist class.

Because they are struggling and developing in a capitalist environment, the unions are exposed to the infiltration of capitalist ideas which confuse the membership and weaken their will to unite and fight in their own interests. That is why every, trade unionist is interested in the building of a powerful Communist Party which will expose all capitalist lies and illusions, and will inspire the whole working class with a militant Socialist spirit.

Only to the extent that an understanding of the grandeur of Socialism grips the masses of the trade unionists can they solve their day-to-day problems and advance to the Socialist society in which "the free development of each is the condition for the free development of all."

Forty Fighting Years: The Communist Record

FORTY YEARS AGO on July 31st and August 1st, 1920, the British Communist Party was born in the midst of the revolutionary crisis which developed towards the end of the first world war. For the first time in the history of the capitalist system socialism appeared to millions of workers as an immediate possibility. The Russian Revolution had proved that the capitalists and the landlords could be overthrown, and the construction of a socialist order of society commenced. With every victory of the Red Army over capitalist intervention the enthusiasm of the active workers grew. The Russian Revolution had been followed by the German Revolution, and although this had been halted, as a result of the treachery of the right-wing Social-Democrats, there were hopes that in this key country of European capitalism the advance might be resumed. At home there was a terrific strike wave. In 1919 the miners had won the seven-hour day and the promise of mines' nationalisation, should a Royal Commission, which had been appointed, pronounce in favour of that policy (a promise that the Government subsequently repudiated). The railways had been reorganised and big wage increases won, and the dockers had obtained an agreement which looked forward to the ending of the blight of casual labour. Associated with the growing militancy, was an increased understanding that the Russian Revolution was a victory for the workers everywhere, and that industrial action must be used to hinder the attempts of the capitalist states, with Britain and France at their head, to destroy the new socialist state. In the East End of London, Harry Pollitt, Mrs. Walker and others, active in the "Hands Off Russia" movement, were carrying out an agitation which culminated in April 1920 in the dockers' refusal to load the *Jolly George* with munitions for Poland.

All over Europe, important, and in some, majority sections of the established Socialist Parties, were beginning to transform themselves into Communist Parties, and were seeking to direct the rapidly rising mass movement. In Britain there was no mass Socialist Party on an individual membership basis, and the militants who were attracted to communism were scattered in propaganda socialist groups of the left like the British Socialist Party, the Socialist Labour Party, the South Wales Communist Council, the left wing of the Independent Labour Party, and groups connected with the wartime shop stewards' movements and the miners' reform movements. It was out of these groups that the cadres and membership of a united Communist Party, capable of giving leadership to the developing mass movement had to come.

The united Communist Party came into existence in three stages. On July 31st and August 1st, 1920, the Communist Party was formed at a conference of delegates from the British Socialist Party, the Communist Unity Group of the Scottish Labour Party, and the South Wales Communist Council. It included such stalwarts of the British working class as Harry Pollitt, Tom Bell, Arthur MacManus, Albert Inkpin, Arthur Horner, William Paul, R. Page Arnot, James Gardner, Isabel Brown, Andrew Rothstein, and Bob Stewart. In January 1921 there was a unity conference with the Workers Socialist Federation and the Communist Labour Party in Scotland (composed mainly of shop stewards' and miners' reform movements grouped around the *Scottish Worker*) in which William Gallacher, J. R. Campbell, and Alec Geddes were prominent members. By the spring of 1921 the left wing of the I.L.P., with Palme Dutt, Emile Burns, Ernest Brown, and Shapurji Saklatvala (later M.P. for North Battersea elected on a Communist policy) came in, and unity was complete.

Employers' Offensive

The united Communist Party had hardly been formed

when the economic crisis of 1921-23 broke out and the growth of mass unemployment encouraged the employers to apply their traditional remedy of wage cuts. The reformist leaders of the railwaymen and transport workers broke up the triple alliance and left the miners to battle, heroically but unsuccessfully against wage cuts. Subsequent to the defeat of the miners every other section of the workers suffered wage cuts.

Such were the circumstances in which the Communist Party had to transform itself from an association of propaganda groups into a militant Communist Party capable of giving the entire working class a lead in its daily struggles, and of pointing the Socialist way forward. Communist principles of organisation and mass work were outlined in a famous commission report from Harry Pollitt, R. Palme Dutt, and Harry Inkpin issued in 1922. It took quite a time and a lot of serious mistakes before the Communist Party organisation began to function. Yet the turn to mass politics, coupled with this organisation, enabled a party of devoted men and women to make a powerful impact on the workers' struggle.

In this pamphlet we can only deal with some of the many occasions when our party influenced masses of the British people to struggle against the might of British monopoly capitalism. We choose, because of their topical interest for the present generation:

I. The struggle against the employers' offensive, which culminated in the General Strike of 1926.

II. The struggle for an alliance of British workers and colonial peoples.

III. The struggle for unity against fascism and war.

IV. The Party in the post-war struggle for peace.

V. The Party in the post-war struggle for a socialist policy for Britain.

113

Towards the General Strike

When the Party commenced this campaign in 1922 under the slogan of "Stop the Retreat" its members were influential in some of the leading trades councils in the country, which were coming together in a federation to discuss common problems. At a district level its members were prominent in a number of important unions. The party organ the *Workers' Weekly* was reaching out to about 40,000 readers per week, being sold mainly in door-to-door canvassing. Everywhere Communist Party members were influential in the rapidly growing National Unemployed Workers' Movement whose leader was Wal Hannington. It was soon realised, however, that if the trade union movement was to beat off further attacks there had to be a closer association between the Communist Party members and the active militants in a number of unions, so in response to this need the National Minority Movement was born in 1924, with William Gallacher and later Harry Pollitt as the Secretary, and the veteran Socialist Tom Mann as the Chairman.

Arthur James Cook, General Secretary of the Miners' Federation of Great Britain, was a member of the movement, and for a time good relations were maintained with a number of members of the General Council of the Trades Union Congress. In 1924 the Communist Party began to establish factory groups, which were immediately encouraged to get out factory papers. These papers besides criticising management policies and personalities put across the party's general industrial and political policy. They were a relatively new thing in British political life and were snapped up eagerly. The workers were determined to force increases of wages, the forty-four-hour week and work or full maintenance for the unemployed. Rank-and-file lefts inside the Labour Party were determined that the next Labour Government would operate a definite socialist policy, as opposed to the spineless wobbling of the 1924 MacDonald Government. In order to unite all these streams of left opinion a Sunday newspaper— the *Sunday Worker*, was formed under Communist influence but drawing—its

114

contributors from the lefts in the General Council of the T.U.C. from a number of left M.P.s, and from local Labour Party activists. At its highest point its circulation was around the 100,000 mark. So despite the numerical weakness of the Communist Party—approximately 4,000 members in 1925—there was a reasonably powerful propaganda machine, influencing many workers and creating a feeling for working class unity in the fight to wrest concessions from the capitalist class and to defeat the Tories.

Towards Red Friday

It was in this situation that the Tories adopted a policy which involved a headlong attack against working class wages. Churchill, then Chancellor of the Exchequer, took the fateful step of putting the pound back on the gold standard while raising its exchange rates. This increased the price of all British exports at the stroke of a pen. Export trade was faced with disaster unless export prices came down and so long as the pound remained overvalued the only way that the capitalist class saw of achieving this was an all-round reduction of wages. The miners who had obtained a slight increase in wages in 1924 were not only faced with a demand for a reduction of wages, but with the replacement of the seven-hour day with the eight-hour day. From every section of the movement came demands for resistance. The miners' case was stated at a special Trades Union Congress on July 24th, 1925, and the following day the General Council of the T.U.C. got the agreement of the railway and transport unions that in the event of a miners' lock-out they would impose a complete embargo on the transport of coal. Faced with unity and with a knowledge of working class determination in every area of the country, the Tory Government surrendered. It induced the mine-owners to withdraw their lock-out notices, and agreed to subsidise the industry up to April 1926, in order that existing wages might be paid. It also set up a Royal Commission, under Sir Herbert Samuel, to investigate the conditions of the mining industry.

Everyone knew that without the tremendous self-sacrificing drive of the Communists and their left allies amongst the rank and file, the irresistible working class pressure, which created the unity of Red Friday, would not have existed.

The Arrest of the Twelve

So the right-wing leader, Ramsay MacDonald decided on a political show-down with the Communists, while the Government prepared to clap the Communist leaders in jail, as a preliminary to a show-down with the entire Labour movement.

At the Labour Party conference in October, 1925, the reactionary forces organised by MacDonald rejected, by an overwhelming vote, a resolution calling for Communist affiliation to the Labour Party and endorsed previous decisions that no Communist could represent his union in any Labour Party organisation, and that no Communist should be allowed to be an individual member of the Labour Party. This was a signal to the Government.

So a few days later it arrested twelve[1] Communist leaders on a charge of "seditious conspiracy". The Government was wise enough not to rest its case on the activity of the accused in organising resistance to wage cuts, but on their dissemination of "seditious" communist literature, (particularly the resolutions of the Communist International), their speeches, and occasional articles. Campbell, Gallacher and Pollitt defended themselves. Five of the prisoners who had previous convictions, Gallacher, Hannington, Inkpin, Pollitt and Rust, were sentenced to twelve months' imprisonment and the others (after rejecting the Judge's offer that they could go free if they renounced their political activity) were sentenced to six months. The sentences did not intimidate the Communist Party. An emergency leadership, which included Bob Stewart, George Hardy, Andrew Rothstein, Aitken Ferguson, and Emile Burns took over, and the entire activity of the Party was intensified. The circulation of the press grew; new members were made. A

116

powerful campaign for the release of the prisoners was launched, in which 300,000 signatures were collected; but the main activity of the Communist Party was to induce the working class movement to prepare for the next round of the struggle.

Agitation in the factories and systematic activity in the trade union branches were increased. The Minority Movement organised a number of local and sectional conferences which led up to a National Conference of Action held on March 1926 at which there were 883 delegates.

The main demands of the Conference were Councils of Action in every town, 100 per cent trade unionism, formation of Workers' Defence Corps, Organisation of Food Departments in touch with the Co-operatives, publication of Strike Bulletins, the summoning of a National Congress of Action to secure full power to the General Council.

Meantime the Government was preparing to crush the movement. A body called the Organisation for the Maintenance of Supplies was formed whose main function, in practice, was to keep the transport system going.

Nine Glorious Days

On the other hand, the General Council of the Trades Union Congress displayed the most bovine passivity. They were hoping that the Samuel Commission would make a number of recommendations which would enable them to wriggle out of their obligation unconditionally to support the miners' resistance. When the Samuel Commission Report came out the General Council slowly moved to a position that involved its acceptance (with its proposals for the rationalisation of the industry), and also the acceptance of some wage cuts by the miners.

Given the tremendous pressure of the working class, the General Council had no alternative but to recommend a

Conference of Trade Union Executives on May 1st, 1926, to call a General Strike for Monday evening, May 3rd, in support of the miners, who were already locked out. They did so not to force the Government and mine-owners to withdraw the demand for wage cuts, but to compromise.

The strike was envisaged to take place in waves. The first wave to be called out were (in addition to the locked-out miners) all transport, printing, heavy industry (iron and steel, metals, heavy chemicals), building (except housing and hospitals). Engineering and shipbuilding workers were to be called out later. A sub-committee of the General Council met the Prime Minister and two colleagues on Saturday, May 1st, and Sunday, May 2nd. From these meetings a formula emerged which had to be taken back for consideration by the General Council of the T.U.C. and the miners.

"We will urge the miners to authorise us to enter upon a decision with the understanding that they and we accept the Report, as the basis of a settlement, *and we approach it with the knowledge that it may involve some reduction in wages.*"

This was the capitulation of 1921 all over again. It was a formula which, if completely rejected by the miners, would have enabled the General Council to call off the strike. But when conversations with the General Council as a whole and the miners were still proceeding the Government struck its first blow. Members of NATSOPA at the *Daily Mail* had refused to print it with an editorial denouncing the strike. The Government asked the General Council to repudiate this and "immediately and unconditionally" withdraw "the instructions for a general strike".

With the tremendous solidarity of the rank and file for the strike, the General Council could not call it off, and so on the evening of May 3rd, 1926, the struggle was on. The T.U.C. admitted that "reports have passed all expectations. Not only the railwaymen and the transport men, but all other trades came out in a manner we did not expect immediately".

Councils of Action

All over the country the Trades Councils immediately formed themselves into Councils of Action or Strike Committees, and sought by mass picketing to ensure that the stoppage was as complete as possible. Over seventy of those local organisations issued duplicated strike or information bulletins, in which the experience of Communist Party branches was often utilised. In addition, many Communist branches got out their own duplicated bulletins and leaflets. Party Centre issued "Workers' Daily" and the "Workers' Bulletin", and in Scotland a duplicated "Worker".

Throughout the whole nine days the General Strike continued unshaken. The B.B.C. afternoon bulletin on May 11th announced "there are no signs of a relaxation of the strike situation as a whole". In the evening bulletin it said, "There is as yet little sign of a collapse of the strike" and on Wednesday, May 12th, "The position as a whole is still one of deadlock".

The General Council was being intimidated by Government allegations that the strike was illegal. They flinched before the workers' demands for a more aggressive strike policy, so on May 12th they decided to call the strike off without even attempting to get any guarantees against victimisation. They pretended that concessions had been won in negotiations with Sir Herbert Samuel, the Chairman of the Coal Commission, but this was false.

The employers, particularly the railway companies, felt that they could afford to victimise; but speedily found out that they were not confronted with a demoralised mass. The workers stood firm and there was aggressive picketing outside all the main depots. In the main the employers had to take the men

119

back without victimisation though they extracted agreements from some unions that they would not, in future, strike without negotiations.

The miners were to fight for another seven months before resuming work. Their magnificent struggle, however, held the capitalist class off from attacking other workers. Wage-cutting had proved to be a very costly thing for the British capitalists' economy. Today the right-wing leaders are fond of declaring that strikes alienate support from their Party. The General Strike had no such effect. It opened the eyes of many workers who broke away from the capitalist parties and supported Labour, despite the shifty, treacherous attitude of its leaders. The Labour vote advanced from 5,500,000 in 1924 to 8,400,000 in 1929.

II

Colonial Workers—Our Allies

From its inception the Communist Party strove to explain to the British workers the nature of monopoly capitalism as a cause of war, of the oppression of colonial peoples and of the intensified exploitation to which the British workers were being subjected in an effort to provide the resources for an extension and strengthening of the power of the British Empire. The Socialist Parties, which were operating before the Communist Party was formed were (with the exception of the Fabians) anti-imperialist in the sense that they opposed wars (like the Boer War) for the expansion of the empire, and looked to freeing the colonial peoples under socialism.

The Communist Party was the first organisation, however, which treated the colonial people as a progressive force in their own right, as allies of the British workers in the struggle against British monopoly capitalism. Gradually the most progressive workers were won to this point of view which found an expression in a successful resolution of the National Amalgamated Furnishing Trades Association at the 1925 T.U.C. This said:

"This Trades Union Congress believes that the domination of non-British peoples by the British Government is a form of capitalist exploitation having for its object the securing for British capitalists (1) of cheap sources of raw materials, (2) the right to exploit cheap and unorganised labour and to use the competition of that labour to degrade the workers' standards in Great Britain.

"It declares its complete opposition to imperialism and resolves (i) to support the workers in all parts of the British Empire to organise the trade unions and political parties to further their interests, and (ii) to support the right of all peoples in the British Empire to self-determination, including the right to choose complete separation from the Empire."

The celebrated Jimmy Thomas, the General Secretary of the National Union of Railwaymen, who was later to rat from the movement, plaintively asked: "Does he [Mr. Purcell, the mover of the resolution] want self-determination for Kenya?" Harry Pollitt, supporting the resolution, said that "imperialism meant the slavery which existed in Kenya at the present time . . . Empire to the whole of the exploited races of the world simply meant that they were being exploited by a set of capitalists. The Indian workers could not hold a strike meeting without being shot".

The Communist Party did not confine itself to pious declarations of support for colonial peoples forming their own political parties and trade unions. It sent some of its members, Percy Glading, the late George Allison, the late Ben Bradley,

121

and Philip Spratt to India to assist in the development of the unions and the Workers' and Peasants' Party. In the famous Meerut Trial of 1929-33, Bradley, Spratt and Lester Hutchinson (a left Labour M.P., 1945-50) stood alongside twenty-nine leaders of Indian trade unionism and of the Workers' and Peasants' Party, charged with organising the struggle of the workers and peasants against inhuman conditions and for struggle against British imperialism.

In the second world war, British Communists on service in India had an opportunity of seeing at first hand the powerful Communist Party which had grown from the small beginnings of a few years previously. Indeed, non-Communist soldiers often made their first contact with Communism through the Indian Communist Party, and returned to Britain to join the Communist Party and fight for the liberation of all colonial peoples.

That struggle still goes on. Although many of the colonies have achieved political independence, they are still in the grip of the imperialists as far as their economic life is concerned; and their struggle together with the British workers in order to achieve complete national freedom has still to be won.

III

Against Fascism and War

From 1926 onwards the capitalist system in Europe began to expand, most of all in Germany, least of all in Britain. Theories of "organised capitalism" alleging that the capitalists now understood how to minimise booms aid slumps were widespread. In the midst of this boastful complacency, the crash of share values on the New York Stock Exchange in the autumn of 1929 reverberated round the world. Mass unemployment, amounting at its height to 25 per cent of the employed population, developed in all industrial countries.

A few months before this crisis broke out the second Labour Government, dependent on Liberal support, was elected, as a "lesser evil" to the hated Toryism. It neither expected the crisis, nor had the faintest idea what to do about it. It dithered while unemployment grew to monstrous proportions, and finally split asunder in the midst of the world-wide financial crisis of 1931.

In 1929 Harry Pollitt, universally acknowledged as the Party's outstanding leader, became General Secretary, and promptly began to reorganise methods of work. A number of new leaders began to come to the front, including William Rust, D. F. Springhall, Ted Bramley, Peter Kerrigan, Idris Cox, John Mahon, Abe and Alex Moffat, Isabel Brown, Marjorie Pollitt, Rose Smith, Joe Scott, George Allison, Claude Berridge and James Shields. On January 1st, 1930, the long-awaited *Daily Worker* came out with William Rust as the editor. Walter Holmes, Allen Hutt, Frank Patterson, were prominent members of the staff in those early days. A new and highly successful phase of the Party's activity had opened.

Here we have only space to deal with the Party's leadership of the British workers in the struggle against fascism which had emerged out of the crisis. For in January 1933 the German monopoly capitalists lifted Adolf Hitler and the Nazi Party to power and initiated the chain of events which led to the second world war. It took some time for the Communist Party to convince masses of the British people that this was no specific German event, and that fascism in various forms threatened the freedom and peace of all mankind.

The right-wing Labour bureaucracy which had blundered so badly in relation to its estimate of capitalist trends proceeded to blunder even more outrageously. Fascism and communism were two forms of dictatorship, they alleged, and the British workers must resist both. On this basis the T.U.C. General Council in 1934 issued Black Circulars suggesting that Communists should not be elected as delegates to Trades

Councils. They also came out against the policy of resisting the activity and provocation of the British Union of Fascists, led by Sir Oswald Mosley (a renegade from the Labour Party).

Unity in Action

But the Communist Party, on the basis of a united front with socialist groups, trades union branches, and trades councils, the local branches of the National Unemployed Workers' Movement, brought masses of workers on to the streets. When Mosley in the autumn of 1934 tried to stage a great demonstration in Hyde Park, it was the Communist Party which was the driving force in the united front group which organised the huge counterdemonstration, behind which Mosley and his supporters skulked, protected by a circle of police.

When Mosley attempted to march through the East End of London in the autumn of 1936, it was the Communist Party which issued the slogan "MOSLEY SHALL NOT PASS". There was a tremendous response on the part of trades councils, trade union branches, and the smaller socialist organisations. The workers set up barricades in Cable Street and the police advised Mosley to call off the march. The right wing, however, kept disdainfully aloof.

From 1933 onwards the Communists were the driving force in the Committee for the Relief of the Victims of Fascism, in which many Labour M.P.s, like Ellen Wilkinson, Sir Stafford Cripps and D. N. Pritt co-operated. Huge meetings and conferences were held all over the country. Thousands of trade union branches, Co-operative Guilds, Trades Councils and local organisations participated.

That fascism led directly to war was underlined when the Italians attacked and annexed Abyssinia in the autumn of 1935, and when Italian and German troops and air force intervened in the attack on the democratically elected Government in Spain in 1936.

The British Government pretended at first to be against the Italian invasion of Abyssinia, and got a League of Nations' decision against Italy. On the basis that it was defending collective security against aggression it launched a powerful campaign in the General Election of 1935. The Communist Party declared that a change of government was necessary if a genuine policy of resistance to fascist aggression was to be operated. In pursuance of its united, front policy it withdrew all its candidates except Harry Pollitt in East Rhondda and William Gallacher in West Fife. Pollitt got over 13,000 votes but could not defeat his right-wing Labour opponent. Gallacher succeeded, however, in defeating Adamson, a notorious right-winger, and for fifteen years fought a tremendous battle for working class unity, peace and socialism, by pointed questions, powerful speeches (not to speak of deadly interruptions) inside Parliament.

The attempt in 1936 on the part of a military-fascist group, headed by General Franco, to dissolve the Spanish Government was at first defeated by the united struggle of the democratic forces, at the head of which stood the Communist Party and the Socialist Party. The rising would have been finally overcome had not the German and Italian Governments sent food, military supplies and men. Hitler sent 50,000, Mussolini sent 110,000, Portugal 20,000 and hundreds of thousands of Moors from Spanish Morocco served in the fascist forces. The fascist war against democracy and national independence had commenced.

The Spanish struggle awakened many British to an understanding that fascism would ultimately attack Britain and an even wider Committee, the National Joint Committee was formed, which had members on it from every political party, from trade unions, from the Co-operative movement and from the various other committees on Spain which were already in existence. The right-wing lie that nobody can work with the Communists was exploded by the united enthusiastic work of these committees, in which well-known Communists like Isabel and Ernest Brown, were amongst the leading spirits.

The British Battalion

One day in the early autumn of 1936 the veteran Socialist H. N. Brailsford called at the Communist Party office to urge Harry Pollitt to begin recruiting a corps of volunteers to go to Spain and fight on the Republican side. To his immense delight he found that the first contingent of British and Irish volunteers had already crossed the Channel.

The British Battalion of the International Brigade was in all the main battles of the Spanish civil war and proved itself to be a hard hitting dependable force. During the life of the Brigade British comrades like Peter Kerrigan, Bill Alexander, D. F. Springhall, Sam Wild, Walter Tapsell, Bert Williams, William Paynter, William Rust and Bob Cooney were active in command. Harry Pollitt visited the battalion five times during the course of the war. One thousand, five hundred men served in its ranks. Five hundred and thirty-three were killed and the majority of the others were wounded at one time or another. One half of the members of the Battalion were Communist Party members as were one half of the dead.

During this period the Communist Party was to participate in one more effort to promote working class unity in the struggle against fascism. Conversations were held with the Socialist League, in which Sir Stafford Cripps, Aneurin Bevan, Barbara Castle, and Michael Foot were prominent members, and the Independent Labour Party with Fenner Brockway, James Maxton, John McNair at the head. An agreement on the lines of the campaign was drawn up and powerful enthusiastic demonstrations were held throughout the country. As usual the right-wing bureaucracy threatened the members of the Socialist League (affiliated to the Labour Party) and the character of the campaign had to be changed to protect these comrades. Nevertheless, the vast anti-fascist activity was having a tremendous effect inside the Labour Party. Local Labour Parties were clamouring for the right to elect their delegates directly to the constituency section of the National Executive Committee, instead of the entire conference, including the trades union delegations with their block votes electing them. At the 1937 Conference at Bournemouth they won this precious right and Sir Stafford Cripps, D. N. Pritt, and Harold Laski were amongst the lefts elected to the N.E.C.

In this period great numbers of middle class and professional people were drawn into the campaigns on behalf of Spain and on behalf of a Popular Front policy. The need for a class alliance of the workers and middle class and professional sections became widely understood. It was the unity campaigns which the bureaucracy opposed, the policy of the class alliance between the working class and middle class and professional sections, which won increasing numbers of the latter for support of the Labour movement and for the Labour Party in the General Elections of 1945.

The Communist Party and its allies played a major part in the struggle to prevent the betrayal of Czechoslovakia which the Chamberlain Government was plotting throughout the summer of 1938. On May 23rd, 1938, a manifesto from the Communist Party said: "The aims of Hitler are directed to making Czechoslovakia a vassal state of Germany, and clear the way for Hitler's war aims in Europe as a whole. These aims are the conquest of Europe and that means Britain as well as Czechoslovakia and France, as well as the Balkan countries and the Soviet Union."

Gallacher Speaks Out

A powerful campaign of meetings and demonstrations for the defence of Czechoslovakia was organised. The *Daily Worker* day after day exposed the trickery of the Chamberlain Government and amidst the disgraceful rejoicing in the British Parliament when Chamberlain was about to depart for Munich, to sign the final act of betrayal, William Gallacher declared:

"No one desires peace more than I and my Party, but peace based on freedom and democracy, and not on the dismemberment and destruction of a small state. It is the policy of the National Government which has led us into this situation." [*Shouts of "No".*]

"Yes, and if we get peace it is the determination of the people that has saved it.

"Whatever the outcome the National Government will have to account for its policy. I am no party to what is going on here. There are many fascists on the other side of the House as in Germany. I object to the sacrifice of Czechoslovakia."

Though the betrayal of Czechoslovakia was carried out and encouraged Hitler to go on to his next victim, Poland, and to precipitate the second world war, it did succeed in convincing great masses of the British people that they were in deadly peril from aggressive fascism and sooner or later Hitler had to be stopped.

The Young Communist League led by John Gollan, William Wainwright, and others, became in this period the most influential youth organisation in the struggle against fascism and war. Prevented by the right-wing bureaucracy from having a formal united front with the Labour League of Youth, the branches of the Y.C.L. and the L.L.Y. engaged in joint work in many localities. A broad alliance was formed with other youth organisations. The Emergency Youth Peace Campaign united the League of Nations Youth Groups, the Young Liberals, the University Labour Federation and the Labour League of Youth in great demonstrations against the threat to Czechoslovakia and other forms of peace and anti-fascist activity. The Y.C.L. also co-operated in the British Youth Peace Assembly in which thirty national organisations of youth were united. *Challenge*, whose first editor was William Wainwright, was built up as the most successful youth paper in the country, with a circulation of 20,000 per week.

Communist groups were active in the universities and worked together with Labour Party members in an endeavour to build the University Labour Federation as the mass organisation uniting all Socialist, Communist and anti-fascist students. George Matthews and James Klugmann are amongst the present leading comrades who were active in this work.

In this period Marxist-Leninist theory, particularly in relation to imperialism, was studied by many active workers and intellectuals. Before the first world war Marxist classics were few and usually badly translated and the infinite richness of Marxism was whittled down to an economic theory. After the formation of the Party the circulation of Marxist-Leninist classics began to increase but it was not until the 1930's that they began to be studied on a really massive scale, as were books by British Marxists like R. P. Arnot, Emile Burns, Christopher Caudwell, Maurice Cornforth, J. R. Campbell, R. P. Dutt, Maurice Dobb, Hyman Fagan, Ralph Fox, William Gallacher, John Gollan, J. B. S. Haldane, Wal Hannington, Allen Hutt, Jack Lindsay, A. L. Morton, John Mahon, Harry Pollitt, George Thomson, Dona Torr and Alick West.

In the latter part of this period the Communist Party and the Communist press began to grow. At the Thirteenth Congress in 1935 it was announced that membership was 6,500; at the Fourteenth Congress in 1937, 12,250; and at the Fifteenth in 1938 there were 15,750. At the time of the Thirteenth Congress (1935) the weekly print of the *Daily Worker* was 180,000; at the Fourteenth (1937), 425,000. In a campaign before the Fourteenth Congress 20,000 new daily readers were won. Some special editions of the paper in this period sold 150,000 copies.

War Breaks Out

Even when it became clear that Hitler was about to attack Poland the Chamberlain Government refused to build an effective political and military front. Under the pressure of public indignation they pretended to be anxious to discuss the formation of a bloc of peaceful states, including the Soviet Union. They even sent a mission of fourth-rate military personalities by slow boat to the Soviet Union, but these had no firm propositions to discuss and it was only too clear that the government still hoped to divert the Nazis against the Soviet Union; and so the Soviet Union, in self-protection, had to sign the Soviet-German non-aggression pact.

The Anglo-French declaration of war in September, 1939, did not basically challenge the aggressive plans of fascism. The aim of the "phoney war" was to force Germany to a compromise in the West and to encourage it to turn East against the Soviet Union. Thus, although France and Britain had superiority in the West, they did not attack, and remained passive when the Germans were over-running Poland.

The capitalist press naturally sought to divert attention away from the British Government's refusal to agree to a bloc with the Soviet Union by denunciation of that state. During the Finnish war it made such bellicose anti-Soviet propaganda that it was clear that a section of the British imperialists, while failing to develop the struggle against the Nazis, were enthusiastic for a war against the Soviet Union. They rushed planes and equipment to Finland and sought Norwegian permission (which was refused) to send a British force across Norway to fight alongside the Finns against the Soviet Union. Indeed, until France and Britain were defeated in the offensive of the Nazis in May, 1940, there were strong elements in both countries who argued that it was necessary to "switch the war" against the Soviet Union.

Throughout this period the Communist Party fought for adequate air raid protection for the people, defended the workers' interests by building up powerful shop stewards' organisations; demanded the suppression of war-profiteering; denounced the repressions in India; combated the anti-Soviet lies and kept the way open for an understanding with the Soviet Union, which was ultimately made possible by the strong resistance trends emerging in Europe and by the warlike hostility of the Nazis to the Soviet Union (which they recognised was an obstacle to their plans), culminating in their declaration of war in June, 1941.

Campaign for Victory

The keynote of the Communist Party's struggle during the great antifascist war was expressed by Harry Pollitt when he said "an anti-fascist war can only be won when the whole resources of the nation are fully utilised and the common people drawn more directly into the whole conduct of the war, alongside the essential measures for social and economic betterment." In a resolution entitled "Britain Today and Tomorrow" the Party outlined a series of important social changes "which we believe that the Government should carry through now, both in order to strengthen the home front for victory and to prepare for after the war." At the same time the Party carried out a ruthless exposure of the imperialist policy of delaying the opening of the Second Front in the hope that the Soviet Union and Nazi Germany would mutually exhaust themselves and that the Western imperialists, winning the war "on the cheap", would establish their predominance after victory.

In combating this imperialist policy the Communist Party carried out a great impressive campaign throughout the country which inspired the masses of British workers with the conviction that the war could be won, the reactionaries in Britain decisively weakened, and a government installed which would bring about sweeping changes after the war.

As the end of the war approached and it became clear that the Tories in the coalition government were about to stage a sudden election, the Party issued the slogan "Clear Out the Tories". It approached the Labour Party with proposals for co-operation to secure a government based on a majority of Labour and Communist M.P.s. This was, as usual, rejected, but at the Labour Party Conference held in Blackpool in May 1945, the Amalgamated Engineering Union and the National Union of Distributive Workers moved that the Conference Arrangements Committee proposals be referred back in order to permit the Conference to discuss "the advisability or otherwise of making an arrangement with the progressive parties at the General Election". The reference back was only lost by 1,314,000 votes to 1,219,000.

The Labour Party won a sweeping victory at the General Election, getting 12 million votes against 10 million for the Tories and their allies the National Liberals and 2,200,000 for the Liberals. The Communist Party ran twenty-one candidates, who got 102,780 votes, and comrades William Gallacher and Phil Piratin were elected to Parliament. There was an especially close contest in Rhondda East, where Harry Pollitt was defeated by 16,733 to 15,761.

IV

Post-War Struggle for Peace

The Labour Party took office in 1945, with vast opportunities confronting it. The fascist powers had been ground into the dust. Their pre-war supporters, the great monopolists of all capitalist lands, had been heavily discredited. A major part in the victory over fascism had been achieved by a socialist great power-the Soviet Union. Where fascist or near-fascist groups had ruled in Eastern Europe, there were now governments controlled by Socialists and Communists. In capitalist Western Europe Socialists and Communists were prominent in nearly every government. The capitalists in Britain, as in Western Europe generally, had no alternative but to make concessions. Major colonies were throwing off the imperialist yoke. The capitalist class of Europe was never in a poorer position to resist working class advance.

The one country in which the capitalist class was still unshaken, the United States of America, had a huge surplus of food and raw materials at its disposal and intended to use it to promote the restoration of capitalism in all Europe west of the Soviet Union. To get Europe in its grip it abruptly terminated the Lease-Lend in 1945. It made a loan to Britain in 1946 but attached a convertibility clause which rendered it completely abortive. It poured its millions into France and Italy and incited the capitalist parties and the Right Socialists to throw the Communists out of the Government. Aided by the British Labour Party it sought to operate the same policy in Czechoslovakia but it was the workers who threw the capitalist parties out and the frustrated Western powers had the audacity to denounce this as an unforgivable example of Communist aggression.

Finally, spurred on by Ernest Bevin, the U.S. formulated the Marshall Plan, whose basic idea was to use American economic and political weight to restore capitalism in Europe. When the Soviet Union and the People's Democracies in Eastern Europe refused to accept it, their decision was denounced as an act of Communist aggression.

Cold War Alliance

The aims of the so-called Anglo-American Alliance were (1) to restore capitalism in Western Europe; (2) to mobilise under the slogan of "containment" all possible force against the Soviet Union; (3) ultimately to "liberate" Eastern Europe by force.

So in 1949 the North Atlantic Treaty Organisation was born and the vicious cold war against the Soviet Union and Eastern Europe was institutionalised. "Negotiation from Strength" was the slogan—which meant that no negotiations with the Soviet Union would be undertaken until the West, which had of course the atom bomb, had built such superiority of strength as to be able to overawe that state. The British economy, struggling desperately to modernise industry and build up foreign trade, was called to face new crushing arms burdens. In 1950 in the midst of the Korean War, military expenditure was increased from £861 million per year to a projected £1,600 million.

It was in this period that the tragic worship of the atom bomb commenced in the Labour movement. Although Britain is one of the states most vulnerable to nuclear warfare, countless Labour speeches were made as if this deadly form of mass murder was of some special advantage to Britain. Peace became a dirty word for many right-wing leaders. Members of the Labour Party taking part in peace organisations, advocating negotiations with the Soviet Union, became liable to expulsion. The final and most disastrous step was taken in 1950. Ernest Bevin landed at the Idlewild Airport in America declaring that Britain still opposed the rearmament of Germany. When he flew out again the Americans had convinced him of its necessity.

In this period the Communist Party sought to win the British people for a policy of "Britain Free and Independent" (1948 Congress).

In the autumn of 1948 the *Daily Worker* organised great peace conferences. In London 1,300 delegates attended, and in Glasgow 600.

The Party began to campaign for:

1. Unconditional prohibition of nuclear weapons and the establishment of strict international control.

2. A peace pact between the U.S.A., Great Britain, China, France and the Soviet Union.

In the spring of 1950 the Party supported the Stockholm Petition for the banning of the H-bomb. Tremendous work was done in door-to-door canvassing, in the market places and in the factories. Hostility had to be overcome, arguments answered, and people persuaded to sign. It was the first large-scale sustained campaign denouncing the employment of this murderous weapon, exposing nuclear strategy and its dangers to all mankind. Over one and a quarter million signatures were collected in favour of the ban.

Korean War

It was inevitable that in the early stages of the Korean War, Party members had to overcome a great deal of ill-feeling, particularly in the factories as the American interpretation of that event was widely accepted. The American attempt to conquer all Korea on behalf of their puppet, Syngman Rhee, and the vicious American hostility to the People's Republic of China was courageously exposed, and so gradually the Party's campaign to end the war by negotiations grew in strength. An especially important role in the struggle for peace in Korea was played by the National Assembly of Women in which Communist Party members united with other progressive women in a valiant struggle for peace. The *Daily Worker*, with its correspondent Alan Winnington on the spot, rendered outstanding service in making the facts about this war widely known.

In the tremendous struggle which went on for a period of several years to induce the Labour movement to abandon its support of German rearmament, the Communist Party members were the driving force in the union branches and the factories, though influential sections of the Labour Party, under the influence of Aneurin Bevan, were in the struggle right from the start. The British Peace Committee mobilised many adherents of peace for this campaign. The right wing played down the dangerous and infamous policy which they were supporting by declaring that all that was being asked for was that Western Germany "should make a contribution to the defence of Europe". When one looks today at the powerful West German army, the strongest army in the capitalist world, next to that of the U.S.A., and when one realises that the American generals are out to arm it with nuclear weapons, then one can only regard the right-wing campaign as one of the most infamous deceptions in all Labour history. A majority of trade union conferences declared their opposition to German rearmament. The Amalgamated Society of Woodworkers' delegation at the Labour Party Conference brushed aside the decision of their annual conference, and voted for it, and the right wing won by 3,270,000 votes to 2,910,000.

Against the H-Bomb

A still more hazardous decision was taken in the spring of 1955 when the Labour opposition declared its support for the Tory decision to manufacture the hydrogen bomb. In the General Election which followed almost immediately after, the Communists were the only party which condemned the decision to manufacture this weapon.

In March 1954 a Japanese fishing vessel, the *Fukuryu Maru* was caught by the fall-out of an American hydrogen bomb test, and the crew suffered terrible injuries through burns. It was a convincing demonstration of the hideous character of the new weapons, and was soon reinforced by the warnings of the scientists that the radiation from these tests was a menace to the human race.

In the autumn of 1957 it was disclosed that U.S. planes, based on Britain, were engaged in flights while carrying H-bombs and were liable to receive orders to proceed against the Soviet Union. The Communist Party conducted a powerful campaign against such flights and demanded the removal of American air bases from this country. A series of demonstrations were held at all the American air bases inside Britain. In addition large peace demonstrations were held in various parts of the country. The Communist Party always linked the campaign against the H-bomb, against H-planes and

136

rocket bases, with the drive for a Summit conference of the heads of government which would clear the way for the settlement of the outstanding questions, which would end the cold war and open the way to peaceful co-existence of states with different social systems.

Early in 1958, the Campaign for Nuclear Disarmament, which was independent of all political parties, was formed. It brought together many people (particularly the youth) who had no connection with the existing political parties, attracted enormous meetings and organised the successful Aldermaston marches.

The Fight for Peace

In 1959 the vast swing of public opinion on the H-bomb was expressed in the growing success of Aldermaston marches and in the declaration of the Annual Conference of the General and Municipal Workers in favour of the renunciation of the H-bomb. Although this decision was subsequently reversed by a special conference, it was an accurate reflection of the development of opinion inside the Labour movement. In the months that followed, the union branches, particularly those in which the Communists and the lefts were active, began to show their appreciation of the fact that a large-scale nuclear war meant not defence but the annihilation of the human race, and therefore as part of a wider peace policy the British Government ought to renounce nuclear weapons now. Important union conferences endorsed this policy.

Point was added to this campaign when it was discovered in 1960 that the Blue Streak rocket which was to convey Britain's hydrogen bomb warheads had already been rendered obsolete by the rocket developments. This completely destroyed the main thesis of Messrs. Gaitskell and Strachey and other British hydrogen bomb worshippers, that the British hydrogen weapons would enable them, in certain circumstances, to act independently of the United States. The right-wing leaders have since, however, demonstrated their continued adherence to the cold war and to N.A.T.O. Let America be the H-bomb state inside N.A.T.O. and let the others supply the conventional weapons—"the poor bloody infantry"—is the basic proposition of their new defence document.

Far be it from us to claim that the Communist Party is the only force for peace in Britain, but there is no denying that its campaigns have played a major part in bringing about an immense change in public opinion in recent years.

The right-wing policy of "no negotiations" with the Soviet Union until that state shows signs of a change of heart has been sunk without trace.

The belief that the Soviet Union is an aggressive power threatening war is discredited amongst the British people. The intransigence of the United States, its consistent refusal to engage in serious negotiations on any questions, the adventurist and aggressive policy pursued by its military leaders exemplified in the concepts of "liberation" (of Eastern Europe) and "massive retaliation" (all-out hydrogen bomb warfare); the contemptuous attitude to allies are provoking increasing resentment amongst the British people.

The building up of the military power of Western Germany is being widely recognised as a disastrous mistake, especially as that state is displaying an attitude of pronounced hostility to Britain.

The folly of nuclear strategy, which means gambling with the very existence of the human race, is being widely recognised.

All this adds up to what the Communist Party has been preaching since 1945-the need for an independent British foreign policy, which throws overboard all vestiges of cold war thought and which bases itself on the interests of the mass of the British people.

Struggle for Socialist Policy

In 1945, the Communist Party was agreed that the Labour Party policy, operated in a democratic fashion, could be a big step forward. It therefore called for the "fulfilment of the Labour electoral programme and full support of the Labour Government for the fulfilment of this programme, including nationalisation of coal and power, transport and iron and steel, a vigorous housing programme, and Mension of health, education and social services".

The Party warned, however, that "entrenched monopoly in Britain resists social and economic change, and demands lowered standards of the working people," in order to promote its aims of trade war and that "within the Labour movement, unity has still to be achieved, and the dangerous influence of, reformism, which opposes unity and surrenders to capitalist policies, has still to be overcome".

The Labour Party economic policy was based on the "mixed economy". A number of basic industries were to be nationalised and private industry was to be subject to a modified system of price and raw material controls, which would enable the government to influence their policy. The monopolies resisted this control policy right from the first. An elaborate system of evasions developed, and step by step the control machinery broke down and the Government was compelled to make a bonfire of controls. Private industry was allowed to raise its prices on the market to the highest possible extent.

Amongst the industries taken into public ownership, railways and coal were technically backward, requiring an enormous outlay for their modernisation. It should have been obvious that they could not (1) meet the interest charges on these new loans and (2) find heavy compensation for the old shareholders. Labour Government policy assumed that they would do both.

At first, price control in both nationalised industries and privately owned industries was assumed. Then price control of goods produced by private enterprise was lifted (except food prices). On the other hand price control in nationalised industries was maintained.

So the nationalised industries had to buy their supplies at full market prices from private enterprise while being competed to sell their own goods and services at less than full market prices, and thus private enterprise was permitted to prey on them. This became the basis for the "failure" of nationalisation, which the Tory Party has made much of in recent years.

Finally, the warning of the Communist Party that huge military expenditure was the enemy of social progress was dramatically justified in the closing months of the Labour Government. The doubling of arms expenditure, in the midst of a powerful spurt of inflation, due to the world-wide arms drive, led to an unprecedented rise in prices, and the sharp reduction of the purchasing power of all wages and salaries. In the General Election of 1951 the Government was defeated.

Throughout the whole of the period of the Labour Government the Communists opposed the reformist policy. The Communist Party put forward a number of measures for reducing the inflationary tension, which included (1) the reduction of the armed forces; (2) more severe limitation of dividends paid, and an annual capital tax on holdings of over £10,000.

End the Wage Freeze

The Communist Party opposed the policy of the wage freeze from its inception, declaring that "living standards have already been reduced by rapidly rising prices". Despite the furious anti-Communist campaign in the unions, a direct product of the cold war, the Communists, supported by masses of trade unionists, fought this infamous policy, until the General Council of the Trades Union Congress was compelled to drop it.

The existing type of nationalisation was criticised. "Only a handful of industries are nationalised, and these are used to provide profits for the former owners and cheap services for the private profit-making industries. This has to be wrung out of the workers of those industries before any improvements are made in their wages and working conditions, or in prices to the general public, while the new capital required to put those industries in order adds new burdens of interest. Neither the people as a whole, nor the workers in those industries can afford to go on paying these huge compensation charges."

In its election programme for the 1950 election the Party showed how the social services were being eroded by the constantly rising prices. "Advance in the social services has been blocked by war policy. The Government in 1949 spent more on war preparations than it did on health, housing, labour, national insurance and grants to local authorities all put together."

Pensions and unemployment and sickness benefit, at 26s. per week, were far too low. "Twenty-six shillings at the present level of prices buys much less than the pre-war benefit (for unemployment and sickness benefit) of 18s. did." An increase of pensions and benefits was demanded.

In 1950, on the insistence of Harry Pollitt, the Party began to discuss its long-term programme, the first draft being prepared by him and John Gollan.

The British Road

The programme—*The British Road to Socialism*—showed how working class unity could attract other sections of the people to united action for peace and for social and democratic advance and could on that basis win a parliamentary majority. This majority, supported by the mass organisations of the people, could transform parliament and the State apparatus into effective instruments of the people's will.

Parliament had existed in different forms, under different social systems, for a period of almost 800 years. It had been a feudal assembly in the Middle Ages, had, during the dissolution of feudalism, been influenced and later dominated and transformed by the rising bourgeoisie. It was now an institution which by and large served the monopoly capitalist system. Nevertheless, *The British Road* insisted, account had to be taken of the fact that this institution had been looked up to throughout English history, by up and coming classes in society.

The programme, therefore, outlined a peaceful road to socialism in accordance with British conditions. This was not merely a matter of securing a majority of the seats in an election. There had to be organised struggle before the election, and the mass organisations of the working class and the people generally had to be prepared to back the parliamentary majority by action outside parliament.

For United Struggle

This could best happen if the working class achieved unity on the basis of a socialist policy and sought to enter into an alliance with other important groups of the population.

So the programme rejected the idea that those groups could not be won for a policy of united struggle on immediate questions of peace, salaries, rents, improvements of social services and defence of the interests of the mass of the people against the encroachments of the monopolists.

It combated the idea that the professional classes could not be won for a socialist policy. Under socialism there would be an enormous expansion of education and much greater opportunities for teachers than there is today. The National Health Service, whose development is being hampered by monopoly capitalism, would be expanded, would be given the best possible facilities and would give much greater opportunities for doctors and health workers than exist today. The intelligent and cultured planning of our towns and cities, which is being frustrated by capitalism, would be undertaken. For the first time in recent history architects would have the possibility of showing what they could do on the basis of large scale comprehensive planning. Socialism would apply science to industry and agriculture, in order in the shortest possible time to raise their productivity. There would be an immense demand for scientists to enable this to be done. There would be public support of all kinds of culture, with the immense opportunities for actors, musicians and other cultural workers.

It was emphasised that there can be no serious politics, which do not take into consideration that Britain is the centre of a world empire in which the oppressed peoples are fighting for, and have in some cases achieved, their political independence, but in which the problems of economic independence and of independent economic development have still to be achieved.

The Communist Party realised that there could be no greater impediment to working class advance, no greater danger to British democracy itself, than for the workers to back imperialist policies and to resent the loss of British rule over the peoples of the empire.

In accordance with this policy the Communist Party has consistently in the teeth of prejudice sought to rally the British people for support of colonial struggles. That was particularly the case in relation to the heroic struggle of the Malayan People's Army and in the independence struggle of the people of Kenya. When Egypt nationalised the Suez Canal the Communist Party was the only party which hailed this as a justified act of liberation. Big sections of the Labour movement repeated Sir Anthony Eden's comparison of Colonel Nasser with Hitler, and Gaitskell suggested economic sanctions. The Communist Party stood firmly by the principle that in a struggle to break the chains that bind it to imperialism the oppressed nation is always right.

The programme recognises that the achievement of political independence by a colonial country is but the first step

143

on the road. The economic heritage of colonial oppression has still to be ended. A socialist government would hand over "all national resources and assets owned by the Crown or British capital in the former colonies to their people".

British industry could play a powerful role in the development of those countries through the technical and economic aid and the supply of machinery and technicians.

> "A socialist government in Britain can seek to promote close, voluntary, fraternal relations for economic, political and cultural co-operation of mutual benefit, on the basis of national independence, equal rights and noninterference in internal affairs between Britain and the former colonial countries, and existing Commonwealth countries, willing to develop such relations".

Socialist Democracy

As revised in 1957, the programme campaigns for a full-fledged socialist democracy as contrasted with the restricted, precariously based "democracy" of present-day capitalism.

The programme guaranteed basic civil rights for all citizens, but it stressed as of even greater importance the everyday functioning of democracy in a socialist society.

The essence of socialist democracy is to replace the control of the rich by participation of the people in running the country, in the work of local government and in the management of industry.

On this basis the unions would not only protect the workers against bureaucratic administration and injustice, but would play a key role in the management of nationalised industries and in the planning organs of society; co-operative organisations would be given greater importance.

That is a genuine socialist democracy, which involves the common ownership of all large-scale industry plus "the participation of the people in running the country".

It has nothing in common with the so-called "democratic socialism" of the right wing, in which democracy is interpreted to mean the dominance of private enterprise, particularly the great monopolies, in the economy.

In the fight for a policy such as that outlined in *The British Road*, united action is essential. Right-wing Labour, seeking to transform the Labour Party into a colourless opposition, accepting all the essentials of capitalism, is the bitter enemy of such unity. Nevertheless, it cannot prevent a great deal of unity at the bottom. Communists and Labour Party workers co-operate in the factories in building up workshop organisation and so improving earnings and working conditions. They co-operate in trade union branches, district committees and national conferences. Indeed, it is the tacit alliance of Communists and the Labour Party militants that is ensuring that the unions will defeat all attempts to abandon the socialist aims of the Labour Party; that they will defeat all attempts to reduce that Party to a corrupt appendage of the Establishment; and that they will, through unity increase the power of the unions, and the working class generally.

All the progressive forces in the Labour movement are handicapped because members of the Communist Party, although they have the complete confidence of their fellow trade unionists, are not allow to represent their union in Constituency Labour Parties or Labour Party Conferences. All who are interested in a genuine socialist policy must unite to sweep aside these bans.

What has been Done

Throughout the forty years the Communist Party has urged the British workers not to tolerate bad conditions of life and work but to fight to change them. Its intervention inspired the workers to resist wage cuts, the unemployed to fight for higher relief, the great mass of the British people to do all in their power to stop the advance of fascism. It was the first to show that the revolt of the colonial people was one of the great liberating movements of our time and the need for the British workers to form an alliance with it. It had faith in the ability of the Russian workers, in the most difficult conditions, to build a socialist society, when large sections of the labour movement in the capitalist world were rejecting that possibility. It has inspired masses of the British people to throw their weight on the side of peace. It has fought to inspire the British workers with faith in themselves and in their ability to achieve a Socialist Britain. In every phase of the British workers' struggle it has given an inspiring constructive lead.

A majority of the working class has been detached from the support of the open capitalist parties, and, despite recent temporary electoral losses due to right-wing policy, this constitutes a powerful political force—a force which if united around a policy challenging the great monopolists could win the overwhelming majority of the British people to its side today. There is, despite right-wing revisionism, a much greater socialist understanding amongst the British workers than in the period between the wars. To that understanding the extensive activity of the Communist Party has contributed.

The trade unions have been built up to their highest point. Amalgamation has reduced the number of unions and the power of workshop organisation has greatly increased. The unions fight on a wider range of issues, not only on wages and hours, but on redundancy, arbitrary dismissals, etc., and make their will known on all the leading political questions of the day. From the 1920's, when it inspired the unions to stop the retreat, the Communist Party has fought for the greatest possible unity in the trade union movement, on the basis of the widest trade union democracy. The hatred of Communist Party members' activity in the trade unions, which in the press of the monopolists is always manifest, is an expression of the importance of this work.

The imperialist outlook of the British workers has been substantially weakened. There is a keener understanding that success for the colonial workers is to the advantage of the British workers. A great deal still remains to be done, but the Communist Party can congratulate itself in playing a major part in bringing about the very great understanding that every advance of the colonial workers is to the advantage of the British worker.

Not only has the hatred of war grown and popular jingoism declined, but the opinion that the working class can influence the course of events is widespread. In the inaugural address to the International Workingmen's Association in 1864 Karl Marx said that events "have taught the working class the duty to master the intricacies of foreign policy; to watch the diplomatic acts of their respective governments; to counteract them if necessary by all means in their power; when unable to prevent war, to combine in simultaneous denunciations, and to vindicate the simple laws of morals and justice, which ought to govern the relations of private individuals, as the rules paramount to the intercourse of nations. The fight for such a foreign policy forms part of the general struggle for the emancipation of the human race." If in a period when peaceful co-existence is possible the British working class is expressing itself more vigorously than ever in the cause of peace, this owes a great deal to the ceaseless activity of the Communist Party.

The furious cold war propaganda, particularly during the period of the Labour Government, was intended to diminish the feeling of the British workers for the Soviet Union; and it had some effect, which was earing off, however, when the exposure of the harmful results of the personality cult at the Twentieth Congress of the Communist Party of the Soviet Union and the counter-revolutionary events in Hungary stimulated a temporary revival. However, the effect of this propaganda is diminishing as intercourse between the British unions and those of the socialist world increase, as cultural exchanges develop, and as the tremendous progress of the socialist world becomes better known. Attempts of the right-wing Labour worshippers of N.A.T.O. and the H-bomb to depict the socialist world as "the enemy" are vehemently rejected.

Many of the militants of the British working class have thoroughly absorbed these lessons. They are resisting all attempts of the right-wing leadership to induce the Labour Party to drop its socialist aims. They seek to preserve these aims not merely as a declaration of principles, but as a guide to the action of the new generation coming into politics. Increasing unity of the left can isolate the right wing and release the vast potential strength of the movement in the fight for socialism in Britain.

The Changed World

Outside Britain the world has changed enormously in these forty years. When the Communist Party was formed, Soviet Russia was defeating the last (the Polish) intervention. The tremendous task of developing socialist industry and agriculture on the basis of the most modern technique and of carrying through the cultural revolution lay in the fixture. Today the Soviet Union is the second industrial power in the world and has set itself the task of surpassing the United States in production and consumption per head. This claim is being taken seriously. American economists and business leaders are admitting that the growth of the American capitalist economy is lagging behind that of the Soviet Union. What Mr. Richard Nixon calls "growth-manship" occupies U.S. business and economic thought.

In Asia the victorious Chinese Revolution is an example to all peoples anxious to throw off age-long backwardness and rapidly to develop their country on the basis of socialist economic planning. No-one doubts that China's advance outpaces by far that of India, where the capitalist (native and foreign) elements in the economy are still strong.

In Eastern Europe, a group of countries—Poland, Rumania, Bulgaria, Hungary, Albania, which before the war were dominated by military-fascist dictatorships, are progressing rapidly on a socialist basis. Balkans and Eastern Europe are no longer synonymous with ignorance and poverty, but with rapid social advance. In the German Democratic Republic (once the home ground of the Junkers) and in Czechoslovakia, in both of which there was already considerable industrialisation, the pace of socialist advance is exceptionally rapid.

In the colonial world the vast liberation movement sweeps aside all obstacles. The imperialists in abandoning direct political control of the colonies sought to control them economically. They cherished the delusion that they were the only sources from which the colonies could obtain economic assistance, and that therefore their economic domination could continue. The existence of the rapidly developing socialist world, able and willing to grant economic and technical aid without strings, is successfully challenging this strategy.

For Socialism and Peace

The socialist world, supported in the main by the ex-colonies, is the mainstay of world peace. Its peace policy is supported by growing numbers of peoples in the capitalist lands. Throughout the world the movement of the peoples to dispel the menace of nuclear war and to secure peaceful co-existence between states based on different social systems, is advancing triumphantly.

In such a world situation the Communist Party is in a better position than it has been for many years, to influence the British people, winning them for a policy of socialism and peace. The fight against the attempts to revise the Labour Party constitution has shown the very strong socialist convictions existing in the working class, and the possibility of building a measure of unity amongst Socialists in the Labour and Trade

149

Union movement. Such a left grouping would have the powerful support of the *Daily Worker*, the only daily newspaper devoted to the political and economic struggle of the British people, applying socialist criticism to monopoly capitalism and pointing the socialist way forward. A rapid increase in the membership of the Communist Party and in the circulation of the *Daily Worker* will give an impetus to the revival of socialist thought and socialist policies throughout the movement.

The British people by their past labours have amassed a vast fund of productive power, of science and technique, and of democratic initiative, which if applied in the service of the people, in this age of automation, can guarantee unheard of prosperity, leisure and opportunities of free development for all.

So on its Fortieth Anniversary the Communist Party, proud of its past contribution to the progress of the British people, invites all who desire to see Britain a prosperous, socialist democracy, participating in worldwide socialist advance, to join its ranks and hasten the achievement of this great goal.

Notes

1. Arthur MacManus (Chairman); William Gallacher (Vice-Chairman); Albert Inkpin (Secretary); Harry Pollitt, J. R. Campbell, Tom Bell, William Rust, J. T. Murphy (members of the Political Bureau); Ernest Cant (London Organiser); Walter Hannington (Secretary of the National Unemployed Workers' Movement); Robin Page Arnot (of the Labour Research Department who had been active in preparing the miners' case, and Tom Wintringham (Assistant Editor of the *Workers' Weekly*). Harry Pollitt was Secretary of the National Minority Movement and J. R. Campbell was Acting Editor of the *Workers' Weekly*. Simultaneously on the instigation of Scotland Yard Palme Dutt was arrested and held in prison in Brussels, with orders to deport him in order to take his place in the trial of the twelve, but an international campaign defeated the deportation order.

www.ingramcontent.com/pod-product-compliance
Lightning Source LLC
Chambersburg PA
CBHW070139290526
45789CB00002B/553